A History of Baton Rouge, 1699–1812

ROSE MEYERS

A History of
Baton Rouge
1699-1812

Published for the Baton Rouge Bicentennial Corporation
by the Louisiana State University Press • Baton Rouge

LIBRARY OF CONGRESS CATALOGING IN PUBLICATION DATA

Meyers, Rose, 1918–
    A history of Baton Rouge, 1699–1812.

    Based on the author's thesis, Louisiana State
University.
    Bibliography: p. 137
    Includes index.
    1. Baton Rouge, La.—History. I. Title.
F379.B33M49   976.3'18   75–27663
ISBN 0–8071–0175–3

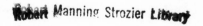

To my husband,
Richard Caswell Meyers, Jr.

Contents

Illustrations

Preface

AN IMPORTANT BY-PRODUCT of the Bicentennial celebration
has been a resurgence of interest in local history. This became
evident to me when housewives, businessmen, students, and
a city council member came to the East Baton Rouge Parish
Library, where I work, to read my master's thesis on the
history of Baton Rouge. Then when members of the Baton
Rouge Bicentennial Commission read the thesis and approved it and the director of the Louisiana State University
Press thought I had the right material at the right time, I
began preparation of a manuscript.

This book surveys the history of Baton Rouge from 1699,
when it was first discovered by the French, to 1812, when it
became a part of the state of Louisiana. It also describes the
international importance of West Florida, the part Baton
Rouge had in the American Revolution, and gives a preview
of territorial expansionism in the United States.

Probably the book is a product of the frequent frustration I
felt when reaching for a book that wasn't there. For years
students came to the library asking for a history of Baton
Rouge, and we gave them bits and pieces from files and
general histories. Exasperation fostered an idea in 1966 when
I was awarded a post-master's fellowship and given leave to
do graduate work in history. The resulting volume is my gift

to all the boys and girls who asked for a history of Baton Rouge.

I owe a debt of gratitude to so many people that I could not possibly name them all. Without their help this book would not have been completed. My deepest gratitude is to Edwin A. Davis who taught me and inspired me to write, saying he would make a historian of me yet, and to Mark T. Carleton for his invaluable guidance in the preparation of my thesis on which the book is based. I am grateful, also, to John Loos for his suggestions, many of which have been used here.

A special thanks is due the Baton Rouge Bicentennial Commission for its financial support and to its chairman, C. Ward Bond, whose enthusiasm for the book gave me confidence in its worth; also to Jo Ann Samuel, a commission member, who supported the project and came by often with words of encouragement after I began the manuscript.

To Charles East, director of the Louisiana State University Press at the time of my writing, goes my unbounded gratitude for his interest over the years in my research. On reading my thesis in 1971, he became interested in its publication, and he worked closely with the Bicentennial Commission in sponsoring the book. His excellent suggestions have added to its historical value and made it more interesting reading. I am grateful also to Martha Lacy Hall, my editor at the Press. Her careful and considerate editing resulted in a smoother and more accurate work.

I would also like to thank Powell A. Casey, military historian, who made many pertinent suggestions that I followed in revising my work. To Tillie Schenker, head librarian, East Baton Rouge Parish Library, who arranged my leave for further study and who has always supported my efforts, and to Margaret Gueymard, former assistant librarian, for her belief in my ability, I give a special, affectionate thank you.

To staff members of libraries and archives in Louisiana, Mississippi, and Alabama, I am grateful; also for a loan system that made material available when I needed it.

Most important of all, I give credit to my family who supported me and showed pride in my work even when they had to deal with a *preoccupied* (my husband's word) wife and mother.

Rose Meyers
Baton Rouge, Louisiana
September, 1975

A History of Baton Rouge, 1699–1812

I

A French Beginning

IN THE SPRING of 1699 Iberville and his men first saw the site on which the city of Baton Rouge is now located. Here they found a lovely land of meadows and wooded areas high on a bluff overlooking the Mississippi River. Situated on the first highlands above the Gulf of Mexico, this site was above the flood level of the Mississippi, which each year inundated lowlands across the river and south of the blufflands.[1] A gentle breeze from the river and a soft subtropical climate made it a very pleasant place indeed.

The chief sign of human life was a little cluster of Indian dwellings roofed with "palmetto leaves, which had been constructed by the Oumas [Houmas], who came here to fish and hunt." Early travelers found that behind the forest line on the river bank there were meadows teeming with wildlife. One of the men in Iberville's party, writing of a later visit to Baton Rouge, said: "Never in my life have I seen such great numbers of buffalo, harts and roes as there were on that Prairie." Birds were plentiful in the tall grass and wooded areas. Turtles, alligators, and fur-bearing animals could be found in the marshy lowlands and bayous at the foot of the hills. A little stream, which emptied into the Mississippi and "resembled a lake" during the spring when the river was

---

1. Andrew C. Albrecht, "The Origin and Early Settlement of Baton Rouge, Louisiana," *Louisiana Historical Quarterly*, XXVIII (January, 1945), 10.

high, was abundantly supplied with fish, including catfish.[2]

This was how the future site of Baton Rouge appeared to French explorers who commenced a written history of the region. There is evidence that men were in the area at least a thousand years before, during the period of the Mound Builders. Two of the mounds built by these ancient inhabitants may still be seen on the campus of Louisiana State University. Another is on the grounds of the State Capitol. In 1699, when Frenchmen appeared on the scene, they found the Houma tribe, which belonged to a linguistic family called the Muskogean group. These Indians occupied the east shore of the Mississippi River north of the Bayagoulas and south of the Natchez Indians, and in 1699 the Houma tribe numbered about 350 families.[3]

While organization of village life was simple—leadership being vested in a chief—the Houmas depended on agriculture, hunting, and fishing for a livelihood. The blufflands of Baton Rouge, where they camped, had a rich soil—"a black light mold about 3 feet deep on the rising ground and between 5 and 6 feet deep in the valleys."[4] Fertile soil, mild temperatures, and an abundance of rain made it easy for the Houmas to plant and harvest a good crop of corn and beans when they came to hunt. Another advantage was ease of transportation; with the Mississippi as the main artery, in addition to the bayous and lesser rivers, travel was easy in any

2. Benjamin F. French (ed.), *Historical Collections of Louisiana and Florida*, Second Series (New York: Albert Mason, 1875), 76; Richebourg Gaillard McWilliams (ed. and trans.), *Fleur de Lys and Calumet; Being the Pénicaut Narrative of French Adventure in Louisiana* (Baton Rouge: Louisiana State University Press, 1953), 81.

3. Albrecht, "Origin and Early Settlement," 29–30; Paul Du Ru, *Journal of Paul Du Ru* (Chicago: Caxton Club, 1934), 7: John R. Swanton, *Indians of the Southeastern United States* (Washington, D.C.: Government Printing Office, 1946), 140, Table I. Swanton gives the population of the Houmas as 600 to 700.

4. Albrecht, "Origin and Early Settlement," 53; A. S. Le Page du Pratz, *The History of Louisiana* (London: T. Becket, 1774), 142–45.

direction one wished to go. And since the Indians were friendly, the site of Baton Rouge would seem to have been an ideal spot for French settlers to establish a colony.

When the French arrived in Louisiana, England and Spain were also interested in colonizing the Mississippi Valley. Spanish explorers presumably saw the site that is now Baton Rouge first. Alonso Alverez de Pineda and his party may have seen the bluffs in 1519, and there is no doubt that after Hernando de Soto's death in 1542 his followers passed the site as they floated down the river to the Gulf of Mexico.[5] But they did not claim this land for their king, nor did they come back to colonize.

Louisiana, which was, of course, much larger than the present state, formally became a French possession in 1682 when René-Robert Cavalier, Sieur de la Salle, claimed it for Louis XIV, king of France.[6] Another sixteen years would go by before the king would commission a French-Canadian, Pierre le Moyne, Sieur d'Iberville, to found a colony in Louisiana.

In 1698 Iberville was assigned two ships, *La Badine* and *Le Marin*, for the voyage to Louisiana. By June, preparations were underway for the expedition; but due to desertions by the crew, Iberville's ill health, and other unavoidable delays, several months passed, and it was September, 1698, before Iberville sailed from La Rochelle, France. Stopping along the way at Brest, Santo Domingo, and Pensacola Bay, he did not drop anchor in Mobile Bay until January 31, 1699.[7]

5. Albrecht, "Origin and Early Settlement," 30–31.
6. Pierre F.-X. de Charlevoix, *History and General Description of New France* (Chicago: Loyola University Press, 1962), III, 213–14; Edwin Adams Davis, *Louisiana: A Narrative History* (Baton Rouge: Claitor's, 1965), 29.
7. Marcel Giraud, *A History of French Louisiana*, trans. Joseph C. Lambert (Baton Rouge: Louisiana State University Press, 1974), I, 23, 31; McWilliams, *Fleur de Lys and Calumet*, 2.

Determined to make a thorough search of the coastline until he found the exact location of the Mississippi River, Iberville carefully chose a party of men to assist in his exploration. Included in this group were young André Pénicaut, a ship's carpenter, and Jean Baptiste le Moyne, Sieur de Bienville, a brother of Iberville. These young men, who were to become very important in the history of Louisiana, were both under twenty years old.[8] Fortunately, a ship's log or journal was kept, which provides historians an official record of the journey up the river and the "discovery" of Baton Rouge.

On February 27 Iberville and his men left the ship in two longboats, and after several days of searching they discovered what they thought was the mouth of the Mississippi, so they decided to go upstream. This journey may well have been hazardous because in March the river is high and the current swift and treacherous. The keeper of the ship's log wrote that after they left the Bayagoulas, going upriver toward the village of the Oumas, the river was "very crooked in this place, with a strong current, and much augmented when the wind is in the same direction."[9]

The explorers had passed Manchacq (Pénicaut's spelling) when they saw the first high land on the Mississippi. Later Pénicaut would describe what he saw in this manner: "From

8. Giraud, *A History of French Louisiana*, I, 31–32; McWilliams (ed. and trans.), *Fleur de Lys and Calumet*, 2; Charles R. Maduell Jr. (comp. and trans.), *The Census Tables for the French Colony of Louisiana from 1699 through 1732* (Baltimore: Genealogical Publishing Co., Inc., 1972), 1–7. Pénicaut included Juchereau de St.-Denis in this expedition, but St.-Denis probably came to Louisiana on Iberville's second voyage. The census taken in December, 1699, does not include him, but the one taken May 25, 1700, lists him as a Canadian officer at Biloxi. Pénicaut also says there were three longboats, but Professor Giraud says there were two, and he is the more reliable.

9. William O. Scroggs, "Origin of the Name of Baton Rouge," *Proceedings of the Historical Society of East and West Baton Rouge, 1916–1917* (Baton Rouge: Louisiana State University, 1917), I, 21; French, *Historical Collections*, 75.

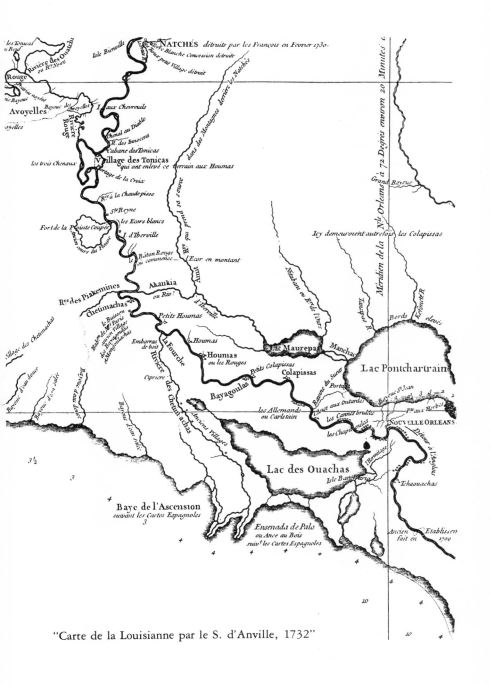

"Carte de la Louisianne par le S. d'Anville, 1732"

there we went five leagues higher and found very high banks called *écorts* in that region, and in savage called *Istrouma* which means red stick, as at this place there is a post painted red that the savages have sunk there to mark the land line between the two nations, namely: land of the Bayagoulas which they were leaving and the land of another nation— thirty leagues upstream from the *baton rouge*—named the Oumas."[10]

Pénicaut first used the words *baton rouge* in a narrative which he completed in 1723. This narrative is the earliest full-length account written by a Frenchman actually participating in the exploration and settlement of Louisiana.[11] Though Pénicaut gives us the name, it is Iberville who gives us the date. They first saw the bluffs of Baton Rouge on March 17, 1699. On that day Iberville saw dwellings covered with palmettos on the east bank of the Mississippi. In his journal, he made the following entry: "On the 17th [of March] we reached a small stream at the right of the river at five and a half leagues from our camp, where they gave us to understand there was a great quantity of fish, and where I had nets stretched and caught only two catfish. . . . This river separates the hunting grounds of the Bayagoulas and the Oumas. Upon its banks are huts covered with palmetto leaves and a reddened Maypole without branches with several heads of fish and bears attached in sacrifice." Another entry for March 17 was made by the keeper of the log of the frigate *Le Marin*. The log (or journal) contains daily entries concerning the trip up the river. This entry states that "At three o'clock in the afternoon we landed near a small stream which was like a lake, and the savages gave us to understand

10. McWilliams (ed. and trans.), *Fleur de Lys and Calumet*, 25.
11. *Ibid.*, xiii.

that it contained many fish. We found here several cabins covered with palmetto leaves, made by the Oumas, who came here to hunt and fish. They had even planted a pole (bois) 30 feet high on which there were heads of fish."[12]

The *baton rouge* the French saw was probably used both as a boundary marker and for ceremonial purposes. It is also probable that Pénicaut's use of the word *Istrouma* was a corruption of the Choctaw word for red pole which was *iti humma*. William Read, after a linguistic study of the origin of the word *Istrouma* accepts Pénicaut's *Istrouma* as meaning red pole.[13]

Locating Pénicaut's *baton rouge* is more difficult because of the number of little rivers or bayous on the Baton Rouge Reach. Historians have differed on this point, citing Bayou Manchac, Bayou Garrison (University Lake), Bayou Monte Sano, Lake Kernan, and Baton Rouge Bayou as possible locations of the red pole. Pénicaut said he found the pole five leagues above Manchac; Iberville says five and a half leagues; and the official log states that they left camp at seven in the morning, and, going upriver against the current, they reached a "small river that resembled a lake at three in the afternoon." This would definitely place the site above Manchac. Also, a 1785 Spanish land grant shows that Margaret O'Brien's concession was in a place called Indian Village near Scott's Bluff with Francis Pousset's land south of Margaret O'Brien's and north of Bayou Monte Sano. It is possible that this Indian Village was the Houma camp. Andrew C. Albrecht, who made a study of all the evidence available to him, wrote that while the site of the red pole

12. Scroggs, "Origin of the Name of Baton Rouge," I, 21, 24.
13. William A. Read, "Istrouma," *Louisiana Historical Quarterly*, XIV (October, 1931), 514–15.

cannot be determined with "absolute certainty," there is enough evidence to make a "scientific claim" that it was near Scott's Bluff.[14]

The story that Baton Rouge was named for a huge cypress tree was started by Le Page du Pratz in his *Histoire de la Louisiane* published in Paris in 1758 and later translated into English in two London editions. He wrote that "Baton Rouge is also on the east side of the Mississippi, and distant twenty-six leagues from New Orleans: it was formerly the grant of M. Artaguette d'Iron: it is there we see the famous cypress-tree of which a ship-carpenter offered to make two pettyaugres, one of sixteen, and the other of fourteen tons. Some one of the first adventurers, who landed in this quarter, happened to say, that tree would make a fine walking-stick, and as cypress is a red wood, it was afterwards called le Baton Rouge. Its height could never be measured, it rises so out of sight." On another occasion, he wrote: "There is a cypress at Baton Rouge . . . which measures twelve yards around, and is of a prodigious height." It appears there may have been Paul Bunyans in Louisiana, too.[15]

Another version of the tree story is: "Having seen nothing but sky and water for months, the warship finally reached the first bluff in the landscape. The captain anchored at the foot of the bluff. When the sun rose, the delighted crew and weary soldiers noticed the different formation of the land. The ship carpenter then espied a huge tree, which made him exclaim in French, "Monsieur le Capitaine, regardez donc ce Joli

14. Albrecht, "Origin and Early Settlement," 35–44, 67. Alcée Fortier and Pierce Butler favor Manchac, and William O. Scroggs says there is only one answer; it is Bayou Garrison which was dammed up to make University Lake. Albrecht believes it was on the bayou part of Lake Kernan.
15. Le Page du Pratz, *History of Louisiana*, 52, 217.

Baton Rouge."[16] So much for historical accounts. Among other things, a longboat had become a French warship. The ship's carpenter, Pénicaut, said they had left the ship in longboats.

Publication of information in Iberville's journal, the ship's log of *Le Marin*, and the Pénicaut narrative leads one to doubt that Baton Rouge was named for a giant cypress tree. Records left by three men who were present on March 17, 1699, when the site of Baton Rouge was discovered, give strength to the argument that the *baton rouge* was a red pole. One can readily believe that it was used as a point of reference by priests, traders, and settlers as they traveled up and down the Mississippi. Significantly, no one was ever able to change the name though it was attempted several times. *Le Baton Rouge* had become a permanent part of the landscape.

No doubt the French explorers were impressed with the climate and bountiful appearance of the land and with the Houmas, who became faithful friends of the French. According to Bienville, the Houmas were glad to share their abundance with white settlers when they were in need.[17] The land was high and dry and would not be inundated when the river rose in the spring. Why, then, were French efforts to settle on this apparently favorable spot doomed to failure? There is no known answer. A curtain seems to drop over these early years of Baton Rouge. History tantalizes us with glimpses here and there—a census record, a name on a map, a brief mention; but that is all, and these glimpses are too brief

---

16. Francis Leon Gassler, *History of St. Joseph's Church* (Marrero, La.: Hope Haven Press, 1943), 2–3.

17. "Memoir on Louisiana by Bienville" in Dunbar Rowland and Allen Godfrey Sanders (eds.), *Mississippi Provincial Archives, 1704–1743. French Dominion* (Jackson: Press of the Mississippi Department of Archives and History, 1932), III, 528.

to tell the story. Who were the first settlers? What were their names? Did they build houses of logs or decide to live in the thatched huts the Houmas found suitable in a mild climate?

Although it is not difficult to find a date for the discovery of the site of Baton Rouge, apparently no one has been able to ascertain an exact date for the founding of a settlement. One writer suggests that a French fort was built there about 1719,[18] and though this date is often given as historical fact, it is doubtful that the fort ever existed.

A land grant called a *concession* was made to a member or members of the Dartaguette family of France. The grant may have originated while Louisiana was still a royal colony, but it is definitely known that it was first settled under the leadership of the Company of the Indies. An entry in Bernard Diron Dartaguette's journal dated December 31, 1722, called the settlement *Dirombourg* or *Baton Rouge*.[19] This was apparently the first attempt to change the name of the settlement, but the more meaningful French for *red stick* survived.

Bernard Diron Dartaguette, who developed the concession at Baton Rouge, was a member of a powerful and influential family. This family would affect the fate of Louisiana for nearly thirty years. At the tender age of thirteen, Bernard Diron Dartaguette came to Louisiana with an older brother,

18. J. St. Clair Favrot, "Baton Rouge, the Historic Capital of Louisiana," *Louisiana Historical Quarterly*, XII (October, 1929), 612. In a later publication Favrot wrote, "There was never a fort at Baton Rouge prior to 1779." See J. St. Clair Favrot, *Tales of Our Town* (Baton Rouge, Louisiana National Bank, 1973), 9.

19. Diron D'Artaguette, "Journal of Diron d'Artaguette" (MS in French copied from the original in Archives des Colonies, Paris), Film 89 in Tulane University Library, New Orleans, La. Nearly everyone who has read this manuscript has called the writer's attention to the spelling of *Dirombourg*, commenting that it must be *Dironbourg*; I have used Dartaguette's spelling. The name *Dartaguette* has been spelled in different ways; Giraud spells it *Dartaguiette*, Dunbar Rowland writes it *d'Artaguette*; in a handwritten manuscript Bienville used *Dartaguette*. There is also some confusion as to whether the name is *Diron Dartaguette* or *Dartaguette Diron*. Martin Dartaguette signed his name simply *Dartaguette* and Bernard Dartaguette signed *Diron*.

Jean-Baptist Martin Dartaguette Diron, who came to investigate a charge of corruption against Governor Bienville by Nicholas de la Salle, the commissary officer.[20] The mere fact that Martin Dartaguette was sent to Louisiana to make the investigation was proof of the confidence the government and the king had in his ability to do the job.

On July 6, 1707, before he embarked on the *Renommee* destined for the Province of Louisiana, Dartaguette wrote the Count de Pontchartrain that he, Dartaguette, required special quarters aboard ship in which to read reports connected with the investigation. The ship's officers felt that he was an ordinary passenger and should not have special quarters, but they were ordered to comply with Dartaguette's request. Martin Dartaguette, after conducting the inquiry, replaced Nicholas de la Salle as Commissary Officer and aided the colony in every way possible. When Dartaguette returned to France in 1711, Bienville wrote that he was one of the "most capable officers I know."[21]

Bienville had been one of the first French visitors to the site of Baton Rouge, and perhaps because of Dartaguette's association with Bienville, the new commissary officer became familiar with the area during the period of his service as a government official in Louisiana (1707–1711). After his return to France, Martin Dartaguette became one of the original directors of the Company of the West in 1717. Either before or shortly after he became a director, he was granted a

20. Jean-Baptiste Martin Dartaguette Diron to Jerome Phelypeaux de Maurepas, count de Pontchartrain, July 6, 1707, in Dunbar Rowland, *Mississippi Provincial Archives*, III, 73–74; Giraud, *A History of French Louisiana*, I, 126, 185. Dartaguette would conduct the investigation with Nicholas De Muy who was coming as governor of Louisiana, but he died enroute and Dartaguette conducted the investigation alone.

21. *Ibid.*, Jean Baptiste Lemoyne, sieur de Bienville to Jerome Phelypeaux de Maurepas, count de Pontchartrain, October 27, 1711, in Dunbar Rowland, *Mississippi Provincial Archives*, III, 168.

concession at Baton Rouge, perhaps jointly with other members of his family. Martin Dartaguette probably never returned to Louisiana. In 1723 he was in France and held the position of tax collector for the district of Auch. André Pénicaut dedicated his book to Dartaguette, possibly seeking favor, since Dartaguette was also a king's counselor and very influential at court.[22]

The second Dartaguette, Captain Bernard Diron Dartaguette, visited the concession at Baton Rouge. He may even have been the actual recipient of the concession, though it was probably granted to the older, more influential member of the family. There was also a third Dartaguette, Pierre Dartaguette, who was captured and burned during the Indian war of 1736.[23] This Dartaguette also visited Baton Rouge, but there is no further mention of him in connection with the concession.

When the first concessionaires of the Company of the West arrived in 1718, Sieur Dugue de Boisbriant, who had been appointed commandant of the Illinois post, accompanied the concessionaires with orders from the company. De Boisbriant ascended the river without delay taking with him Diron Dartaguette and Pierre Dartaguette "both brothers of the former Commissaire Ordonnateur." They visited the Baton Rouge concession and described it as a *tres bien placee* with "2 whites and 25 negroes." By 1722 it was reported that half the concession was burned over and that rice and vegetables had been harvested. The same report said that they had tried to increase the fields and that "there are in this concession

22. McWilliams, *Fleur de Lys and Calumet*, 120, and the Dedication, n. p.

23. Pierre François-Xavier de Charlevoix, *History and General Description of New France* (Chicago: Loyola University Press, 1962), VI, 121. This is a reprint of a six-volume translation by John Gilmary Shea published between 1866 and 1872. The original *Histoire de la Nouvelle France* was published by Charlevoix in France in 1743. The Charlevoix and the Shea editions are now rare books.

about thirty whites and twenty negroes and two Indian slaves." Another census dated May 13, 1722, says "BATON ROUGE, Concession of DIRON, Habitants: ten men, 5 women, 2 children."[24] No mention was made of slaves in this count.

Diron Dartaguette reported that the soil was "very fine and good" and that there were "many prairies" on the concession.[25] Good soil and prairie land would seem to indicate that the acreage under cultivation could be increased with a minimum amount of labor. Settlers would not have to uproot so many trees to clear land as had often been the case. Everything seemed to favor the development of this concession. Thus in less than a quarter of a century after the site that would be called Baton Rouge was discovered by Iberville, a handful of settlers, Frenchmen, blacks and Indians, had made a beginning.

Perhaps most important of all for good Catholics, the year began with the blessing of the Church, a Mass having been celebrated in the home of Diron Dartaguette on New Year's Day, 1722. Father Pierre Franç9is-Xavier de Charlevoix officiated.[26] It is possible that there were earlier blessings at this site and that French priests visited the Houmas not once but many times, but one cannot be certain.

As early as 1698 the Mission of the Seminary of Quebec on the Mississippi was established, and Father François Jolliet de Montigny was appointed superior and vicar general. He set

24. *Ibid.*, 41. Pierre Dartaguette is sometimes referred to as the Chevalier Dartaguette. Emile Lauvrière, *Histoire de la Louisiane Française, 1673–1939* (Baton Rouge: Louisiana State University Press, 1940), 265; William Beer, "Early Census Tables of Louisiana," *Louisiana Historical Quarterly*, XIII (April, 1930), 223; Maduell (comp. and trans.), *The Census Tables for the Colony of Louisiana from 1699 through 1732*, 28. The capital letters were written as found.

25. Beer, "Early Census Tables of Louisiana," XIII, 223.

26. Roger Baudier, *The Catholic Church in Louisiana* (New Orleans: A. W. Hyatt, 1939), 45–46; Gassler, *History of St. Joseph's Church*, 1.

14

Pierre le Moyne, Sieur d'Iberville

out with two other priests for missions on the Mississippi, and one of his companions was Father Antoine Davion, who would later become the beloved missionary to the Tunica Indians.[27] He may have worked with the Houmas, also.

Father Davion's work with the Tunicas began the same year that Iberville visited the Houma Indians at Baton Rouge. Davion's party arrived at Biloxi in July, 1699, and it was on the way down the river from Illinois that "they learned from the Houmas that there were French settlements on the coast." After resting several days at Biloxi, they left "to take possession of the mission of the Tunicas." Marcel

27. Charlevoix, *History and General Description of New France*, V, 129–30.

Gireau wrote that Davion "never lost contact with the tribe; he followed it even in its migrations." Although he worked with other tribes, he was most attached to the Tunicas. The feeling was mutual, because in 1704, when Davion tried to retire from his work with the Tunicas, the chiefs of the tribe went to Mobile to beg him to return.[28]

It is entirely possible that Davion visited the Houmas as he traveled up and down the river during the many years he labored in Louisiana (1699–1722). The Houmas were already noted for their friendliness at this early date. Charlevoix wrote that they had received Iberville "with great cordiality." Another historian wrote that "When the Tunicas came to live with the Houmas, he [Davion] was probably in the section now included in the Feliciana parishes which was a part of the land of the Houmas extending down to Baton Rouge."[29] However, Davion may never have visited the site, though such a visit is certainly within the realm of probability.

Father Pierre François-Xavier de Charlevoix, an adventurous Jesuit priest and scholar, did visit the concession. In 1720 he was sent by the French government to gather information about Louisiana. Governor Vaudrieul of Louisiana and the intendant, Michel Begon, were ordered to furnish him with two canoes, eight companions, and ample supplies. The clever Charlevoix hinted in a letter to a friend that it was much less expensive to send a priest. Originally an officer and fifty men had been made ready, but "the Duc d'Orleans felt that this voyage would entail too great an expense. . . . I

28. Jean-Baptiste Bernard de la Harpe, *Historical Journal of the Settlement of the French in Louisiana* (Lafayette: University of Southwestern Louisiana, 1971), 22–23, 68–69; Giraud, *A History of French Louisiana*, I, 54–56, 337.

29. Charlevoix, *History and General Description of New France*, V, 122; Baudier, *The Catholic Church in Louisiana*, 22.

have been chosen for the task." Furthermore, a priest would be less likely to arouse suspicion. During Charlevoix's exploration of the Mississippi Valley, he visited the Dartaguette concession and on New Year's Day, 1722, celebrated what was perhaps the first official mass in Baton Rouge.[30]

The settlement of Baton Rouge seemed to be well underway in 1722. The Indians were friendly, the first crops had been harvested, the soil was fertile and the climate favorable, and the year had begun with the blessing of the Church. By this time, Diron Dartaguette, inspector general of the troops and militia of the province of Louisiana, probably had high hopes for this venture.[31] But it failed. Why it failed is all the more incredible, because the Dartaguette family was so influential—surely the inspector general of Louisiana could get the necessary supplies, equipment, and troops for the protection of the concession. No less than three members of the family were involved in the development of Louisiana at this time, and one was a counselor at Court in France.

But when Father Paul du Poisson camped overnight at Baton Rouge on June 4, 1727, he found that the settlement had been abandoned. Of this visit he wrote: "On the 4th we slept at Baton Rouge: this is the place named thus because a tree painted red by the savages is there, and which serves the Tribes that are above and below it as a boundary in hunting. Here we found the remains of a French habitation, abandoned on account of wild animals—deer, rabbits, wild cats and bears—that had laid waste everything." That little was done to protect the concession seems evident; "not one of the

---

30. Charlevoix, *History and General Description of New France*, Introductory Biography, I, n. p.; Baudier, *The Catholic Church in Louisiana*, 45–46.
31. Beer, "Early Census Tables," XIII, 214.

sixteen French companies which were distributed throughout the colony in 1722 was stationed at Baton Rouge."[32]

Chevalier de Loubois was supposed to have received
military reinforcements at Baton Rouge when he went to
avenge the Natchez massacre, which took place in 1729.
Whether Loubois did receive reinforcements is debatable,
but it is apparent that by this time Baton Rouge had become
only a geographical point of reference for people who traveled
the Mississippi River. A 1732 map by S. d'Anville shows the
location of "Le Baton Rouge" or "the red stick." A later map
of the Province de la Louisianne, dated 1743, does not show
Baton Rouge at all, though it indicates that Pointe Coupee
on the west bank of the river north of Baton Rouge was a
good-sized settlement by that time. A census taken in 1745
gave the population of Pointe Coupee as two hundred whites
and four hundred blacks. Again there was no mention of
Baton Rouge.[33]

What happened to the Dartaguette concession at Baton
Rouge? Because of lack of evidence, one can only guess.
Perhaps it really was abandoned because of wild animals, as
suggested by Father du Poisson. Disease and death could also
have been causes. J. Hanno Deiler wrote that "such a fearful
epidemic raged in Biloxi among the immigrants that the

32. Reuben Gold Thwaites (ed.), *The Jesuit Relations and Allied Documents: Travels and Explorations of the Jesuit Missionaries in New France, 1610–1791* (Cleveland: Burrows Brothers, 1896–1901), LXVII, 303; Albrecht, "Origin and Early Settlement," XXVIII, 64.

33. "Baton Rouge" from the Old File, National Archives. Copy in State Land Office, Baton Rouge. Le Page du Pratz states that Loubois "went up the river with a small army, and arrived at the Tonicas." He does not say that he stopped at Baton Rouge (p. 83). Charlevoix also notes that the French army assembled at the Tonicas (VI, 95). "Carte de la Louisianne par le S. D'Anville, 1732" (map in Louisiana Room, Louisiana State University Library, Baton Rouge); "Province de la Louisianne, 1743" (map in Louisiana Room, Louisiana State University Library, Baton Rouge); Gayarré, *History of Louisiana*, II, 28.

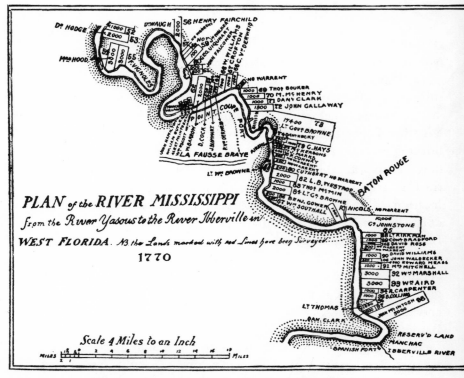

Portion of a map in Dunbar Rowland, *The Official and Statistical Register of the State of Mississippi*

priests at that place, having so many other functions to perform, were no longer able to keep the death register."[34]

However, it is more likely that the venture failed because of what Deiler calls "the criminal neglect of the Compagnie des Indies." Lack of supplies and labor became critical. Dartaguette complained that more than half of the working men and *engagés* (people brought over under service contracts) were dying on the barren coast of the Gulf of Mexico while

34. J. Hanno Deiler, *The Settlement of the German Coast of Louisiana and Creoles of German Descent* (Philadelphia: Americana Germanica Press, 1909), 22–23.

they waited to be sent up the river to concessions. They often stayed there until their supplies were used up or sold. He added that navigation of the Mississippi was very easy and pointed out that Charlevoix had gone down the river in 1722. And, of course, Bienville, who knew that an English vessel carrying sixteen guns had gone up the river in 1699, "repeatedly demanded that these immigrants should not be landed on the gulf coast at all, but should be taken up the Mississippi river. . . ." The directors of the company did not agree with Bienville.[35]

Father Charlevoix wrote that "so many thousand men were left to waste with misery and disease under the pretext that there were not batteaux enough to transport them to their destination, when the very ships that brought them from France might have landed them at New Orleans and even nearer to their concessions." He added that when those in charge finally thought of sounding the mouth of the Mississippi, they found there was sixteen feet of water on the bar! Dartaguette, too, had insisted that the same vessels which brought them from France might just as easily have taken the immigrants to their concessions. As it was, the need for supplies, livestock, and laborers at the site of the concessions became ever more critical.[36]

However, this does not explain how the concession at Pointe Coupee could prosper while the Dartaguette concession at Baton Rouge failed. Supplies had to pass Baton Rouge to reach Pointe Coupee. According to Father du Poisson, wild animals had caused Baton Rouge to be abandoned, but these same wild animals were also native to Pointe Coupee.

35. *Ibid.*, 22–24; Beer, "Early Census Tables," XIII, 227–28.
36. Charlevoix, *History and General Description of New France*, VI, 40.

The concession at Baton Rouge simply dropped from sight. Perhaps somewhere in France there are records that will yet shed light on this mystery. The early history of Baton Rouge has almost a "lost colony" quality—one can only guess.

Thus ends the French period—a strange and bewildering end, to say the least. But better times were coming, and Baton Rouge would come back to life and begin to flourish as the New Richmond settlement under English rule.[37]

37. Eron Rowland, *Life, Letters and Papers of William Dunbar* (Jackson: Press of the Mississippi Historical Society, 1930), 23, 28, 66; William Bartram, *Travels Through North & South Carolina, Georgia, East & West Florida* (Philadelphia: James & Johnson, 1791), 429.

II

Under the
Union Jack

WHEREAS WE HAVE taken into royal consideration the extensive and valuable acquisitions in America, secured to our crown by the late definitive treaty of peace concluded at Paris the tenth day of February last . . . West Florida, bounded to the Southward by the Gulph [*sic*] of Mexico, including all islands within six leagues of the coast from the river Apalachicola to lake Ponchartrain [*sic*]; to the Westward by the said lake, the lake Maurepas, and the river Missippi [*sic*]; to the Northward, by a line drawn East from that part of the river Missippi [*sic*] which lies in 31 degrees North latitude, to the river Apalachicola . . . and to the Eastward by said river.[1]

Thus spoke George III in a proclamation on October 7, 1763, when a government for West Florida was created. Baton Rouge, abandoned, unimportant, a tiny dot on the vast expanse of the North American continent, had passed into the hands of the mightiest nation in the world. By the Treaty of Paris, which ended the Seven Years' War in 1763, Great Britain had "acquired from Spain both East and West Florida and from France that portion of Louisiana north of the Isle of Orleans and East of the Mississippi."[2]

Great Britain, with the world's most powerful navy at her

1. "British Proclamation of October 7, 1763," *Louisiana Historical Quarterly*, XIII (October, 1930), 611.
2. *Ibid.*; Thomas Andrew Bailey, *A Diplomatic History of the American People* (New York: Appleton-Century-Crofts, 1964), 26; Edwin Adams Davis, *Louisiana: A Narrative History* (Baton Rouge: Claitor's, 1965), 97.

command, lost no time in taking possession of the new territory. A government was set up on October 7, and on October 20 Major Robert Farmar of the Thirty-fourth Regiment and commander of His Britannic Majesty's troops in Louisiana issued a manifesto saying that all inhabitants of West Florida were subject to the laws of England. Residents who took the oath of allegiance to King George would be protected "in their property and their religion." This proclamation was read in all the churches and posted on all church doors and other public places. Truly, as Charles Gayarré wrote later, "the British Lion had at last put his paw on a considerable portion of Louisiana."[3] While Spain delayed sending a governor to Spanish Louisiana, the British moved into the Floridas as quickly as possible.

As a result of the Treaty of Paris, navigation of the Mississippi River was "declared to be free to the subjects of either sovereign, in its whole breadth and length, from the source to the sea."[4] No longer, therefore, could British vessels be stopped at New Orleans; they had a legal right to go up the river to their new posts at Manchac, Baton Rouge, and Natchez.

The British also made plans to build a strong new fort in West Florida. Until this could be accomplished, frigates were anchored at Manchac and Natchez. It was especially important to have some kind of defense at Manchac because Bayou Manchac (which appears on early maps as the Iberville River) was the southern boundary of West Florida at this point with Spanish Louisiana on the other side. Bayou Man-

3. Dunbar Rowland, *Mississippi Provincial Archives, 1763–1766; English Dominion* (Nashville Tenn.: Press of Brandon Co., 1911), I, 61–63; Charles Étienne Arthur Gayarré, *History of Louisiana* (Reprint; Gretna, La.: Pelican Publishing Co., 1965), II, 94.

4. François-Xavier Martin, *The History of Louisiana from the Earliest Period* (Reprint; Gretna, La.: Pelican Publishing Co., 1963), 193.

chac, though shallow, was navigable, possibly only in the spring, when it became eight to twenty-one feet deep. Approximately fifty feet wide near the Mississippi, the bayou increased in width to about two hundred eighty feet near Lake Maurepas. Major Farmar ordered Captain James Campbell to clear the channel to the Mississippi. With the help of fifty blacks, he was able to complete the project in about six months. The British also planned to dig a canal from the Mississippi to a deeper part of Bayou Manchac, but these plans failed to materialize.[5] Even without the canal, Bayou Manchac would prove its worth to the planters and businessmen of the area.

An early English map, dated January, 1767, gives the location of a "stockade" Spanish fort in a cleared area south of Bayou Manchac; the English Fort Bute was directly across the bayou. Engineer Archibald Robertson supervised the planning and construction of Fort Bute which consisted of a "blockhouse with a small Stockaded Fort." It housed fifty men and one officer, but, in an emergency, it could be made to accomodate two hundred. Early in 1765 building material had been shipped to Manchac, and by August the fort was apparently ready for occupancy because at this time a detachment was sent to man the fort.[6]

Plans were also drawn for a "New Town" north of Bayou Manchac with wide streets that would divide the area into eighteen blocks. Several redoubts, or forts, were to be placed at strategic points. One redoubt would enclose the church opposite the "Center of the Town," and another would be

5. Gayarré, *History of Louisiana*, II, 123; Map of Iberville River, 1767, State Archives and Records Commission, Baton Rouge, original in British Museum; George Johnston to John Lindsay from Mobile, December 10, 1764, and George Johnston to John Pawnell in Dunbar Rowland, *Mississippi Provincial Archives*, I, 262–63, 271, 358.

6. Map, 1767. State Archives and Records Commission, Baton Rouge, La.

placed "to protect the proposed Cut and defend the Passage of the river." Redoubts of lesser size would protect the "Flanks of the Town." Governor Peter Chester, who laid out the New Town in 1770, was enthusiastic about the area, but political changes in Great Britain and war with Spain, which resulted in the Spanish conquest of West Florida, prevented the development of the town. One would like to think that these elaborate plans were made for the site of Baton Rouge, but nowhere do the plans mention Baton Rouge or New Richmond; yet when the British occupied Baton Rouge, it was, according to Gayarré, "nothing better than a miserable fortlet, and some huts which were scattered about in its neighborhood."[7]

Due to the influence of Lord Bute, George Johnstone, a Scotsman and captain in the Royal Navy, was appointed governor of West Florida in 1763. The governor immediately ordered detachments to the various military posts in West Florida. Major Loftus, with a force of four hundred men, attempted to go up the Mississippi to Illinois, but he met with resistance from Indians and decided to return to Bayou Manchac; he went from there to New Orleans where he boarded a ship for Pensacola. This was in March, 1764, and it was October, 1765, before another English officer, Captain Thomas Sterling, and his Highlanders finally arrived in Illinois.[8]

With West Florida in British hands, smuggling, which

7. Cecil Johnson, "Distribution of Land in British West Florida," *Louisiana Historical Quarterly*, XVI (October, 1933), 547; Gayarré, *History of Louisiana*, II, 125; Map, "Plan for the Proposed New Town, also the Proposed Cut from the Mississippi to the Iberville."

8. Martin, *History of Louisiana*, 194, 195; James A. Padgett, "Commission, Orders and Instructions Issued to George Johnstone, British Governor of West Florida, 1763–1767," *Louisiana Historical Quarterly*, XXI (October, 1938), 1022; Dunbar Rowland, *History of Mississippi* (Jackson: S. J. Clarke Publishing Co., 1925), I, 260.

had always been a problem, now became rampant. Bayou
Manchac had been cleared in 1764, and, according to Governor Johnston, vessels drawing six feet of water could proceed with ease beginning about the middle of January when
the river would begin to rise. British vessels, on the pretext
of going to Manchac, brought goods to planters in Spanish
Louisiana and also gave them good prices for their products.
Consequently, as smuggling increased, economic conditions
improved. The improved economy may also have been due to
the fact that Fort Bute provided protection where Bayou
Manchac joined the Mississippi River; this enabled traders to
bring slaves, who were the main source of wealth for many
planters, into the Baton Rouge area. Blacks were brought
from Pensacola by way of the lakes to Bayou Manchac and
from there to Baton Rouge. Population increased rapidly,
with slaves becoming nearly as numerous as whites.[9]

Having monopolized trade in this area (they even traded
just above New Orleans), the British built a large warehouse
at Baton Rouge which became a depot for contraband. They
went even further when they converted two vessels into floating stores with shelves and counters. According to Gayarré,
they moved these ships up and down the river, stopping "at
every man's door and tempting him and his family in this
indirect way." Until the appointment of Bernardo de Gálvez
as acting governor of Spanish Louisiana in 1777, when the
Spanish were finally permitted to trade legally with the British, Spanish governors simply closed their eyes to illicit trad-
ing because of the economic upsurge.[10] Baton Rouge may

9. George Johnston to John Lindsay, in Dunbar Rowland, *Mississippi Provincial Archives*, I, 263; Davis, *Louisiana: A Narrative History*, 97, 98; Martin, *History of Louisiana*,
196.

10. Davis, *Louisiana: A Narrative History*, 109; Gayarré, *History of Louisiana*, III, 45.

not have succeeded as the Dartaguette concession but as a commercial center and under the plantation system, as the British knew it, the settlement developed rapidly.

At first the government of Baton Rouge and of all West Florida under the British was military. Governor George Johnstone, though appointed in 1763, was unable to take office until he arrived at Pensacola late in 1764. In the interim, Major Robert Farmar, who took possession of the territory on October 20, 1763, administered the civil and military affairs of West Florida.[11] Even before Major Farmar raised the British flag (to the music of bagpipes), King George had issued a proclamation organizing a government for West Florida.

The Proclamation of October 7, 1763, stated that the colonists were to enjoy the rights and benefits of English law. In electing representatives to an Assembly, each household would have one vote. Citizens also had the right of appeal from court decisions.[12] This representative type of government was typically English and very different from the undemocratic governments of Spanish and French Louisiana. The individual became important; moreover, this type of government would appeal to English and American settlers who were coming into Baton Rouge.

The first session of the Assembly of West Florida convened on November 3, 1766, and lasted until January 3, 1767. Francis Pousset was chosen Speaker of the Assembly; and, as Speaker, he demanded the "Usual Privileges"—freedom of speech and debate, the right to call a session in any case of

11. Dunbar Rowland, *History of Mississippi*, I, 253–54.
12. "British Proclamation," 611–12.

emergency, exemption from arrest during the session and access to the governor. These were rights Englishmen had come to think of as "usual," but for much of the world this was not so. It is interesting to note that Francis Pousset was from the District of Mobile in which Baton Rouge was located. His plantation was north of Bayou Monte Sano. Other representatives from this district were Daniel Clark, Henry Lizars, John McGillevray, Daniel Ward and Dougal Campbell.[13]

During this first session of the Assembly a number of acts were passed—regulating trade, encouraging foreigners to settle in West Florida, regulating taverns, and controlling drunkenness, among others. One of the most important acts established the Court of Common Pleas. After signing the bills, Governor Johnstone made a speech and the assembly was adjourned. A copy of two articles in the treaty of peace which pertained to the Floridas was entered in the Journal of the session. It is interesting to note that this treaty granted Roman Catholics the right to practice their religion if they chose to stay in West Florida.[14]

Parts of His Majesty's proclamation of October 7 were also entered in the *Journal*. This proclamation authorized Governor Johnstone to make grants of land to the officers and men who had fought in the French and Indian War. The grants were to be made without fee, and the men were to be exempt for ten years from a quit rent. The size of the grants varied from five thousand acres for a field officer to fifty for a private. The grants stimulated "the settlement of Baton

13. "Minutes of the First Session of the Assembly of West Florida," *Louisiana Historical Quarterly*, XXII (April, 1939), 312–17.

14. *Ibid.*, 375–77.

Rouge and the Feliciana districts." Civilians were also allowed to settle in West Florida, and many large estates in this region can trace their grants back to Johnstone and his successors.[15]

The British government made certain requirements of each settler. He had to build at least one dwelling no smaller than twenty feet in length and sixteen feet in breadth. For every fifty acres of "plantable" land he was required to cultivate three acres, or, if the land was swampy, he had to drain three acres. As for "barren" or pasture land, he had to keep at least three "neat cattle" on every fifty acres. There was a tax of one-half penny sterling per acre to be paid on the Feast of St. Michael. Settlers were exempt from this tax for the first two years. No recipient of a land grant was allowed to leave it undeveloped; the government wisely insisted that it must be improved. Colonists poured into Baton Rouge and other parts of West Florida, and by 1766, when Governor Johnstone resigned, the British colony was in excellent condition.[16]

Lieutenant Governor Montefort Brown, who had a large grant of land near Port Hudson on the Mississippi and north of Baton Rouge, succeeded Governor Johnstone. John Eliot, appointed governor in 1768, committed suicide before he could take office, so Governor Brown continued to serve until 1769. Then Elias Durnford was made acting governor until

15. *Ibid.*, 380; Garnie William McGinty, *A History of Louisiana* (New York: Exposition Press, 1951), 80.

16. "West Florida—Documents Covering a Royal Land Grant and Other Land Transactions on the Mississippi and Amite Rivers during the English Rule," *Louisiana Historical Quarterly*, XII (October, 1929), 630–37; Davis: *Louisiana: A Narrative History*, 110–11; Padgett, "Commission and Orders," 1022–24. Governor Johnstone's administration was characterized by civil and military dissension and by his own personal quarrels with other officials. When he asked for a leave of six months it was understood that he would not return.

the arrival of Peter Chester, who was appointed governor in 1770.[17]

One historian tells us that British adventurers made the most of the fact that land was easy to come by above Manchac and in the Baton Rouge area. A man could obtain a vessel in Jamaica for five hundred dollars. He could buy slaves and goods on credit. When he arrived in West Florida, he could dispose of some of the slaves and supplies and pay for the hire of the vessel. With the remainder of the slaves, he could start a plantation and obtain more supplies on credit until he could make a crop. Within a few years he could become a planter in "easy circumstances."[18]

William Dunbar, who became a very important landowner in Louisiana and Mississippi, is a good example of how one could begin with comparatively little and become a very wealthy man. Dunbar, often called Sir William Dunbar, was born in 1749, the youngest son of Sir Archibald Dunbar of Morayshire, Scotland. Educated in Glasgow, he later went to London to study astronomy and mathematics. He came to America for his health in 1771. By 1773, apparently in good health, he came down the Mississippi on a flatboat to New Richmond (Baton Rouge), and, finding that the land was fertile and the region "very beautiful," he decided to settle there and become a planter. He went to Pensacola to obtain a land grant from Governor Chester, and from there he sailed to Jamaica to buy slaves. He returned to New Richmond by way of the lakes and Bayou Manchac.[19]

Dunbar left a daily account of plantation life in a diary

17. John F. H. Claiborne, *Mississippi, as a Province, Territory, and State* (Baton Rouge: Louisiana State University Press, 1964), 106; Dunbar Rowland, *History of Mississippi*, I, 262–65.

18. Martin, *History of Louisiana*, 217.

19. Eron Rowland, *Life, Letters and Papers of William Dunbar*, 9–10.

William Dunbar. (Courtesy of Mississippi Department of Archives and History)

which he began in May, 1776. He had been on his plantation several years, and at this time he owned slaves of whom seven men and four women were field hands. There were also four women who were house servants. Dunbar writes in his diary that there were twenty-three other "New Negroes" for sale and that they too worked on the plantation. With the help of his slaves, he planted corn, rice, indigo, and pumpkins among other things. But this canny Scot soon found that making and shipping staves would be an excellent source of income. They made staves nearly every day, and he wrote that "we generally fetch in about 3000 a day. He also wrote that he put "on board Phillips' Schooner 22 M 5 C [22,500] staves and heading to be delivered to Campbell at New Orleans." Other entries in his diary tell about his slave sales. Sometimes he would just comment "Sold two Negroes," but occasionally he would give more specific details. On May 29, 1776, he wrote, "Sold one new Negro to Mr. Poupet for . . . 270 Dollars paya. in Decr. next—." Then on Friday, June 7, 1776, he wrote, "Sold McIntosh by desire of Campbell 5 Negroes @ 260 Dol."[20]

Thus a plantation society, based on slave labor, grew up in Baton Rouge and the Felicianas where plantation owners lived in comfort and even in luxury. As war between Great Britain and the thirteen colonies became imminent, planters from the eastern seaboard sought refuge in West Florida. Among the immigrants were many families of wealth and

20. *Ibid.*, 23–24, 48. Dunbar's diary gives many details of the Richmond settlement. He doesn't call it New Richmond. He says "Mississippi Richd. Settlement" and once he writes No. Richmond. More often he speaks of the Richmond Settlement or of the Gentlemen of the Settlement. These gentlemen met regularly to conduct the business of the area. And they did this over dinner and wine. Often they stayed overnight to visit. They bought supplies from Pointe Coupee, and they also borrowed from each other. Dunbar was a pioneer scientist in the South, and he and his friends often discussed science. He entertained William Bartram, the naturalist. Dunbar was a member of the American Philosophical Society.

distinction "who were either loyal in sentiment, or desired to be neutral."[21] To be either had become increasingly difficult, often impossible, in their former home.

While Baton Rouge, or as Dunbar called it the "Mississippi Richmond Settlement," flourished for a dozen or so years under British rule, American colonies on the Atlantic seaboard had become more restive under successive policies of Crown and Parliament. Colonial grievances ultimately resulted in the Declaration of Independence in 1776. Many Englishmen of the Baton Rouge area were in a peculiar position—though they sympathized with their English kinsmen in the thirteen colonies, in West Florida they had never experienced oppression. Compared to Spanish citizens in Louisiana, English settlers had much for which to be thankful, and they feared the consequences of removing the "British Lion" from this area. A very powerful Spanish colony just a few miles south of Baton Rouge was ready to pounce on the relatively defenseless English. Baton Rougeans enjoyed their rights and privileges as English citizens and had no desire to become vassals of a Spanish monarch. If the English in Baton Rouge were fearful, they had a good reason—Spanish agents were already active in West Florida, and Governor Bernardo de Gálvez of Spanish Louisiana was secretly helping the rebelling American colonists with money and supplies. Working through Oliver Pollock, American agent in New Orleans, he seized every opportunity to support the colonists and to suppress British trade.[22]

Captain James Willing, formerly an unsuccessful merchant in Natchez, came down the Mississippi from Fort Pitt,

21. John F. H. Claiborne, *Mississippi as a Province, Territory and State*, 115.

22. James Alton James, *Oliver Pollock: The Life and Times of an Unknown Patriot* (Reprint; Freeport, N.Y.: Books for Libraries Press, 1970), 74–75, 336, 351.

on the Ohio, to New Orleans in 1777. He attempted to persuade England's fourteenth colony—West Florida—to join the struggle for independence. Despite his appeals, the people remained steadfast in their attachment to the Royal Cause.[23] Willing was entertained graciously in the homes of planters, but they simply had no complaint against the king of England. He had given them large grants of land which had made them wealthy. They also had a representative form of government which rested lightly on their shoulders.

Chagrined, Willing returned to Congress with a report that West Florida was a serious threat to the cause of independence. He was commissioned to take a well-armed force and return to West Florida to demand that West Floridians take an oath of neutrality.[24] In January of 1778 he raided British plantations up and down the Mississippi. He captured a vessel at Fort Bute while fifty or sixty men at the fort sought refuge on the Spanish side of the river. Charles Gayarré wrote:

> The Americans proceeded up the river to Baton Rouge, stopping at the several plantations on the way, burning all the houses and other buildings, and carrying off the negroes. A good many of the British planters, on hearing of the approach of these unwelcome visitors, crossed the Mississippi with their most valuable effects and slaves, and sheltered themselves under the Spanish flag, which floated on the right side of the river. . . . The invaders continued up as far as Natchez in their course of devastation, laying waste plantations, destroying the stock, applying the torch of the incendiary to the edifices, and carrying off such slaves as had not followed their masters in their flight.[25]

23. Martin, *History of Louisiana*, 223–24.

24. John F. H. Claiborne, *Mississippi as a Province, Territory and State*, 117–18; Davis, *Louisiana: A Narrative History*, 112–13; Gayarré, *History of Louisiana*, III, 113–14; Dunbar Rowland, *History of Mississippi*, I, 271.

25. Gayarré, *History of Louisiana*, III, 113–14.

William Dunbar, whose plantation was near Baton Rouge and who was personally involved in the Willing raid, wrote a most interesting account of what actually took place during the hectic days when the war first came to Baton Rouge. After the raid was over and from a safe spot across the river, he wrote: "In the Accadian Country, May 1st, 1778. A Grand Revolution hath taken place upon the English side of the Mississippi since the latter End of February which has prevented me from keeping my Journall [sic] these two months past, of which I now come to give some accot [sic]." Then he describes in graphic terms the plundering of Willing's marauders.

Dunbar wrote that he reacted immediately on receiving a report that the Americans had arrived at Manchac and taken over an armed vessel anchored there. He was so alarmed that he hastened to send his slaves under cover of darkness to the Spanish side of the Mississippi River. After seeing his slaves safely hidden, he went immediately to Manchac to see if the reports he had received were true. Not only had the ship been captured but there were also more rumors that as many as five to eight thousand Americans were coming. Then he left for Pointe Coupee taking only what was necessary for the trip. "Not suspecting," he wrote, "that any mischief was intended to the peaceable inhabitants."[26]

At Pointe Coupee, a Mr. Alexander, who had also escaped with his slaves, said that Willing intended, with few exceptions, to plunder every English plantation that had anything of value and that he had a list of those to be given special treatment. Dunbar, Williams, and Pouppet were among

26. John F. H. Claiborne, *Mississippi as a Province, Territory, and State*, 119–20; Eron Rowland, *Life, Letters and Papers of William Dunbar*, 60–63.

those on the list. When the Americans could find no slaves on the English side at Baton Rouge, they crossed the river to Spanish territory and seized the slaves of Pouppet and Marshall. Dunbar wrote that his slaves had been put at a considerable distance from the river and were not discovered by the marauders. But the houses of "English gentlemen," including his, were plundered. Dunbar was robbed of everything that could be carried away—wearing apparel, bed and table linen, and silverware. Not even a shirt was left in the house. He was also robbed of about two hundred pounds sterling. Willing's men destroyed bottled wine, burned businesses, and shot cattle and hogs.

Ironically, Dunbar returned to his home to find that Willing had left a passport for his safety and that of his slaves "until further orders." He set out for New Orleans to see what could be done about this plundering, and on the way he passed two boats headed up the river. These boats reached Baton Rouge, and the plantations of Williams, Watts, and Dicas were raided. Dunbar wrote in his account that all three were made prisoners, "with all their Negroes, notwithstanding that these gentlemen had every assurance of protection and safety, (&) in consequence had taken oaths of newtrality [*sic*]. Villains, Rascalls [*sic*]. Twould be a prostitution of the name of American to honor them with such an apellation. They were all brought to town soon after my arrival and a public Vendue soon commenced of the plundered effects—." Names of others who lost property were Walker, Dutton, Castle, and Harry Stuart. At Walker's they wantonly killed the livestock, burned houses, and destroyed his indigo works. Dutton, of the Plains, lost all his slaves, and his staves were burned "by which the poor man is reduced to the lowest

Ebb of poverty with a family of small children." Dunbar also comments that "Profit & Nash were spared."[27]

Captain Willing plunged into excesses in New Orleans, and when he needed more funds, he simply sent his men up the river again. It has been estimated that he and his men took property valued up to $1,500,000.[28]

After this experience, the British sent more troops to Manchac and other fortified posts along the Mississippi. On July 1, 1778, Dunbar noted in his diary that troops had arrived at Manchac from Pensacola. They established a virtual blockade of the river.[29] These were unsettled times for the people of Baton Rouge, who were caught between opposing forces. It appeared that West Florida would be a battleground for a war that many of them had tried to escape by leaving the thirteen colonies.

Spain formally declared war on Great Britain in June, 1779. Young Governor Bernardo de Gálvez anticipating that war was coming, had prepared for the defense of Louisiana and for an invasion of West Florida when the time was right. Agents stationed throughout the Floridas had kept him informed as to the strengths and weaknesses of the British. Rumors had been circulated that the British would attack Louisiana, but Gálvez wanted to be prepared to strike the first blow when war was declared.[30] He reasoned that the best defense is a good offense particularly if he could attack before the enemy invaded Louisiana.

Gálvez assembled an army of every class, nation, and

27. Eron Rowland, *Life, Letters and Papers of William Dunbar*, 60–63. One wonders if "Pouppett" was the same as the Francis Pousset elected to the first West Florida Assembly.

28. Davis, *Louisiana: A Narrative History*, 113.

29. John Walton Caughey, *Bernardo de Gálvez in Louisiana, 1776–1783* (Berkeley: University of California Press, 1934), 124–25.

30. Davis, *Louisiana: A Narrative History*, 113–15.

color. "It was composed of 170 veteran soldiers, 330 recruits recently arrived from Mexico and the Canary Islands, 20 carabiniers, 60 militiamen and habitants, 80 free Blacks and Mulattoes, and seven American volunteers." The American agent Oliver Pollock was an aide-de-camp to Gálvez throughout the campaign. Men continued to volunteer until Gálvez commanded an army of 1,427 officers and men. The march from New Orleans to Baton Rouge began on August 27, 1779. Many of the men became ill before they reached Fort Bute, but they were able to take the fort by surprise on September 7, 1779. Fort Bute had been guarded by only 26 officers and men. One officer and 5 men escaped; one man was killed and the rest were taken prisoner.[31]

There was a shortage of soldiers at Fort Bute because the main body of troops had been ordered to Baton Rouge where the British were expected to make their stand. Fort Bute, which had originally been built in 1765 primarily to protect workers who were clearing the channel of Bayou Manchac, had been previously abandoned in 1768. Lieutenant Colonel Alexander Dickson, who was in command of the British forces in the Baton Rouge District in 1779, now considered Fort Bute indefensible against cannon. In a letter written at Baton Rouge on September 22, 1779, he explained his reasons for abandoning Fort Bute at this time. It was only after he had consulted with his engineer, F. F. Graham, and other officers who unanimously agreed that the fort at Manchac could not be defended that he sought another spot. Dickson then decided that the Watts and Flowers' plantation at Baton Rouge would be the best place to make a stand.

31. Henry E. Chambers, *A History of Louisiana* (New York: American Historical Society, Inc., 1925), I, 326; Caughey, *Bernardo de Gálvez in Louisiana*, 153–55; Jack D. L. Holmes, *The 1779 "Marcha de Galvez"* (Baton Rouge Bicentennial Corporation, 1974), 12–15.

Dickson sent Graham with a letter asking permission to build a redoubt there, and the owners agreed. As soon as it was feasible, they moved troops, artillery, and stores to the new redoubt. This is the fort often called Fort New Richmond. It was also called the Baton Rouge Redoubt by Lieutenant Colonel Dickson.[32]

In the six weeks preceding hostilities, the British had prepared a formidable fortification. The fort was "surrounded by a ditch eighteen feet wide and nine feet deep. Inside the ditch was an earthen wall and outside it a circle of palisades in the form of a *chevaux de frise*." The fort was armed with thirteen cannon and manned with four hundred regular troops and about one hundred armed civilians, including armed blacks.[33]

Taking stock of the military situation, Gálvez realized that it would be too costly to try to take the fort by assault. He had only ten cannon and fourteen artillerymen, and most of his army consisted of a motley crew of untrained civilians. It would be better to try to out-maneuver the British through military strategy. He was successful and this maneuver was "the tactical climax of his lower Mississippi campaign."

At first glance, a small wooded area seemed the obvious place from which to launch an attack; so Gálvez sent a detachment of black, white, and Indian troops into the area. They chopped down trees and in general made as much commotion as they could. The deception worked beautifully, and the British commenced firing in that direction.[34]

In the meantime, Gálvez quietly installed his artillery on

32. Dunbar Rowland, *History of Mississippi*, I, 260; Johnson, "Distribution of Land," 547; "West Florida—The Capture of Baton Rouge by Gálvez, September 21st, 1779," *Louisiana Historical Quarterly*, XII (April, 1929), 263; Holmes, *Marcha de Gálvez*, 17.

33. Caughey, *Bernardo de Gálvez*, 155–56.

34. Gayarré, *History of Louisiana*, III, 128.

the opposite side of the fort. On September 21 the Spanish began bombarding the fort. Gálvez's strategy was successful, and the damage they were able to inflict was so severe that by midafternoon the English were ready to surrender. At three-thirty in the afternoon they capitulated.[35] In a letter dated September 22, 1779, Dickson wrote: "Early on the morning of the 21st a battery of heavy cannon was opened against it (the fort); and after incessant fire on both sides for more than three hours, I found myself obliged to yield to the great superiority of his artillery, and to surrender the redoubt to his Excellency Don Bernardo de Galvez, who commanded the troops of his Catholic Majesty."[36]

The Spanish commander took full advantage of his position as victor and demanded not only the surrender of Fort New Richmond but also Fort Panmure at Natchez. He then allowed the English twenty-four hours in which to bury their dead; the next afternoon they marched out of the fort and formally surrendered. Three hundred and seventy-five military prisoners were taken, but blacks and settlers were allowed to go free.[37]

In his report to Major General John Campbell, in which he included copies of the Articles of Capitulation, Dickson wrote that "the terms are honorable to the troops and favorable to the inhabitants." He added "that the officers and soldiers . . . are treated with the greatest generosity and attention, not only by the officers, but even the Spanish soldiers seem to take pleasure in being civil and kind to the prisoners."[38]

35. Caughey, *Bernardo de Gálvez*, 157.
36. "West Florida—The Capture of Baton Rouge by Gálvez," 263.
37. Caughey, *Bernardo de Gálvez*, 157.
38. "West Florida—The Capture of Baton Rouge by Gálvez," 257–58.

In the Articles of Capitulation, Dickson had proposed that his men not be made prisoners of war. Gálvez replied that he could not accede to this proposition. He said:

> I therefore positively require their surrendering themselves prisoners of war; but considering the honourable defense made by Lieutenanat-Colonel Dickson, his officers and troops, they shall go out with drums beating, pieces charged, and colours flying, five hundred paces from the fort, where they shall deliver the arms and colours to the troops under my command, and surrender themselves prisoners of war, to be exchanged at the pleasure of the King my Master; engaging, at the same time that they shall be treated with respect and all possible humanity—the field officers shall wear their swords.[39]

It is interesting to note that the Articles were "stipulated in the French language, having no interpreter of the Spanish language in the Fort of Baton Rouge."[40]

Winning the Battle of Baton Rouge in 1779 was an extremely important victory for Gálvez. The surrender of the British commander, Lieutenant Colonel Alexander Dickson, was tantamount to a complete surrender of the Mississippi Valley below Natchez. The success of this campaign encouraged Gálvez to attempt a Gulf Coast campaign. He was victorious again in 1780 and 1781 when both Mobile and Pensacola fell before his onslaught. Even George Washington, preoccupied as he must have been at this time, took time out to write a letter of congratulation, and the King of Spain, when granting many other honors, also promoted Gálvez to the position of captain general of Louisiana and the Floridas.[41]

39. *Ibid.*, 259.
40. *Ibid.*, 257.
41. Davis, *Louisiana: A Narrative History*, 115–18. Among other titles given him by the king of Spain, one finds Conde de Gálvez, Viscount of Gálveztown, Knight Pensioner of the Royal and Distinguished Order of Carlos III.

One reads often of the French contribution to American independence, but not so often of the very substantial contribution made by the Spanish. The conquest of Baton Rouge, Mobile, and Pensacola by the daring young Governor Gálvez of Louisiana was most important to Americans in the Revolutionary War. With the Spanish in control along the Gulf Coast, there was little danger of a British invasion from that direction. Supplies, much needed by the colonists, could move more freely through the gulf and up the river. And last, but far from least, was the loss of prestige by the British among the Indians. According to one Louisiana historian, this loss of prestige "immeasurably aided George Rogers Clark in consolidating his control of the Old Northwest."[42]

Thus ended British control of West Florida. The Post of Baton Rouge had flourished under English administration— the "miserable fortlet" of the French (according to Gayarré) had become a military post of importance surrounded by a thriving plantation economy. Although the British controlled Baton Rouge for only a few years, 1763–1779, their influence on its destiny was far out of proportion to the time spent there. Baton Rouge had become an Anglo-Saxon pocket in Latin Louisiana, and the Anglo-Saxon love of democracy would linger in the hearts of Baton Rougeans and West Floridians of British ancestry. Certain basic rights were dear to them—freedom to worship as they pleased, to elect representatives to a governing body, and to be tried in their own courts. West Floridians never willingly relinquished these rights, and this proved to be disastrous for the Spanish in West Florida.

42. *Ibid*. Other accounts of the Battle of Baton Rouge may be found in titles listed in the bibliography. See Charles Gayarré, François-Xavier Martin, Albert Phelps, and Jack D. H. Holmes. For a more detailed account, see John Walton Caughey.

III

Conquered by Spain

BATON ROUGE NOW passed into the hands of the Spanish. Alexander Dickson's capitulation after the first Battle of Baton Rouge was a severe blow to Major General Campbell. In a letter to Lord George Germain, dated December 15, 1779, Campbell said: "What a grievous mortification must it be to me to have to relate to your Lordship, for my Sovereign's information, the conquest of the Western part of this province, by the arms of Spain, in consequence of their early intelligence of the commencement of hostilities."[1] The quick, decisive military victory of Bernardo de Gálvez at Baton Rouge was only the first of three successive blows that would send the British reeling from the Floridas forever and mortify Major General Campbell even more grievously.

After the surrender of Fort New Richmond at Baton Rouge, Don Carlos de Grand Pré, who had taken part in the surrender of the forts at Thompson's Creek and on the Amite River, was given command of the District of Baton Rouge. Don Pedro Jose Favrot was appointed commandant of the Post of Baton Rouge. On September 25, 1779, a civil decree was issued which required the people of Baton Rouge to take an oath of loyalty to the Spanish king. Residents had six days

---

1. "West Florida—The Capture of Baton Rouge by Gálvez," 256.

in which to comply.[2] This was very distasteful to loyal subjects of King George III. They had already suffered considerable loss of property when they refused to take an oath of neutrality demanded by the Americans. However, this time, having been conquered by Spanish military forces, they had no choice.

Gálvez was a gracious and even generous conqueror, and he tried to reassure the people by declaring that the residents would retain "the full and entire possession of all their effects and slaves, and in short, of everything that belongs to them . . . there shall not be the least insult offered to the troops of the garrison . . . [and] no papers whether public or private, shall be seized searched, or examined under any pretence whatever."[3] In spite of these and other assurances, the people of the District of Baton Rouge, being predominantly Anglo-Saxon and Protestant, were still fearful of the rule of His Catholic Majesty, Carlos III. Within a few weeks an English officer managed to escape with letters and papers for Colonel Dickson. Gálvez ordered Favrot to assemble the people of Baton Rouge and to warn them that they would be punished if they were caught harboring any person in the service of the British king.[4]

Constant rumors about the war kept residents in a state of turmoil. In November, 1779, twenty men were supposed to have left Mobile on horseback headed toward posts on the Mississippi River. Gálvez again urged Favrot to take the

2. Caughey, *Bernardo de Gálvez*, 159; Wilbert James Miller, "The Spanish Commandant of Baton Rouge, 1779–1795" (M.A. thesis, Louisiana State University, Baton Rouge, 1965), 15.

3. Davis, *Louisiana: A Narrative History*, 115; "West Florida—The Capture of Baton Rouge by Gálvez," 260–61.

4. Miller, "The Spanish Commandant," 19–20.

necessary precautions, and if these men came into the Baton Rouge District, to capture them. Some British citizens urged insurrection. One of the agitators toward this end was Robert Ross, and Favrot warned residents not to hide him. In 1781 Ross's goods were confiscated by the Spanish government and sold at public auction.[5]

In April, 1780, the threat of another uprising caused concern at Baton Rouge. Fort Panmure at Natchez had surrendered to the Spanish when Baton Rouge was taken in September, 1779. Within a few months the Spanish became aware of unrest and possible conspiracy among English settlers in the vicinity of Natchez. Pedro Piernas, acting governor of Louisiana, ordered Favrot to send someone to investigate. The commandant did as he was ordered and reported his findings to the governor. Gálvez, on his return, acknowledged the report and stated that Colonel Anthony Hutchins, an Englishman who had escaped from the Spanish, was capable of conspiracy and that the Spanish commandant at Natchez was not taking proper precautions to prevent an uprising.[6]

Then, in the spring of 1781, the people of Natchez did rebel, although they, too, had taken an oath of allegiance to the king of Spain. Captain John Blomart, a Natchez mill owner, led settlers and Indians in an attack against Fort Panmure. The Spanish commandant, Juan de la Villebeuvre, surrendered, and he and his seventy-six men were sent to Baton Rouge. Captain Carlos de Grand Pré moved his militia north from Baton Rouge and *Punta Cortada* (Pointe Coupee). By this time, news of the surrender of Pensacola to Gálvez had reached Natchez. Knowing they could no longer expect

5. *Ibid.*, 21.
6. *Ibid.*, 21-22.

Bernardo de Gálvez. (From the collection of
the Louisiana State Museum)

help from Pensacola, the people of Natchez became terri-fied.[7] Many British residents so feared Spanish retribution for rebellion that they fled into the wilderness.

The rebellion was short lived. On orders of Grand Pré, Spanish forces began to move toward Natchez. With Captain Estavan Roberto de la Morandier in command, they landed on June 22, 1781, met with no opposition, and the fort sur-rendered the next day.[8]

Don Pedro Jose Favrot served as commandant of the Post of Baton Rouge during these crucial years from 1779 to 1781. With the American Revolution still in progress, his first duty was to make sure Fort New Richmond, or Fort San Carlos as it was now called, was militarily adequate in case of attack by the British and their Indian allies. The star-shaped fort was much in need of repairs, especially after the recent bombardment by the Spanish. Favrot proceeded to repair the fort at a cost of 2,472 pesos over the next two years.[9]

Due in large measure to a change in commercial policy, Baton Rouge was to cost the Spanish government a great deal more. England had encouraged a sort of every-man-for-himself policy. British plantation owners and traders had been free to trade with whom they pleased—even if they did so illegally. Commerce flourished from 1763 to 1779 under English rule, but Spain's restrictive mercantilistic policies tended to stifle trade. Spanish colonists were limited to trad-ing with the mother country. (Occasionally, these regula-

7. Caughey, *Bernardo de Gálvez*, 217, 218; Jack D. L. Holmes, *Gayoso: The Life of a Spanish Governor in the Mississippi Valley, 1779–1799* (Baton Rouge: Louisiana State University Press, 1965), 17.

8. Holmes, *Gayoso*, 17; Caughey, *Bernardo de Gálvez*, 220.

9. Miller, *"The Spanish Commandant,"* 16–17. The Spanish fort is now the State Capitol grounds.

tions were lifted when the colonies were in desperate need.) As a result of this policy, Spanish Louisiana never had a favorable trade balance, and the government had to make up the difference in cash. When the value of exports became less than the value of imports, it became necessary for the Spanish government to subsidize the colony—at one time to the extent of 500,000 pesos annually for colonial Louisiana. Much of this money found its way into the hands of merchants who took it out of the colony.[10]

Baton Rouge, along with other posts, became a financial burden to Spain. Salaries for government officials were generally in arrears, sometimes as much as three years. The Post of Baton Rouge had many government employees—surgeon, curate, sacristan, storekeeper, baker, blacksmith, and others of less importance. Copies of original Spanish documents in the Library of Congress give salaries for the Post of Baton Rouge:

	pesos per month
Storehouse Keeper General	30
Surgeon of the Royal Hospital	30
Orderly of the Royal Hospital (several)	15
Curate of the Parish of Baton Rouge	40
Sacristan of Baton Rouge	15
Baker	15
Master Blacksmith and Gunsmith	25

Back salaries for three years amounted to a goodly sum when the Spanish government finally got around to paying these employees.[11]

10. A. P. Nasatir (ed.), "Government Employees and Salaries in Spanish Louisiana," *Louisiana Historical Quarterly*, XXIX (October, 1946), 886.

11. *Ibid.*, 962, 887, 1015–1021. Drafts on the royal treasury were made in 1802 for the purpose of paying salaries for parts of 1799, 1800, and 1801.

In addition to these expenses, money was needed for strictly military purposes. In the year 1780, for example, Baton Rouge averaged one captain, three sergeants and forty-six enlisted men, all of whom cost almost six hundred pesos for the year. In the light of these expenses, there was some discussion as to whether it was feasible to continue the upkeep of Fort San Carlos at Baton Rouge, even though it was being repaired at this time. Esteban Miró, colonel of the Regiment of Infantry of Louisiana, suggested abandonment of the fort. Gálvez disagreed, saying that Fort San Carlos was important because it could repel attacks from the north and that it had advantage as a place of refuge.[12]

The government of Baton Rouge was very different in Spanish West Florida from what it had been under English rule. No longer did residents elect representatives and meet in assembly to govern themselves. Now the laws of the whole province of Louisiana were based on the *Nueva Recopilación de Castile* and the *Recopilación de las Indias*. To make these laws more understandable, two of the governor's legal aides made a digest of the two Spanish codes; the result was the famous Code O'Reilly. This and the French *Code Noir* contained the laws which governed the province.[13]

A triune form of government existed under the Spanish. The executive department had, first of all, the king of Spain, who was supreme; next in power came the captain general of Cuba; then the governor of Louisiana; the commandant of the district or post; and, finally, the syndic or justice of the peace who governed the subdistricts. The position of the Spanish commandant in Louisiana was an adaptation of French provincial government, and very often the Spanish governor

12. Miller, "The Spanish Commandant," 17–19.
13. Chambers, *A History of Louisiana*, I, 301; Martin, *The History of Louisiana*, 214.

appointed Frenchmen to serve as officials. As to the legislative function, laws were made in Spain, but mandates could come from the captain general, from the governor, or from the *audencia* of Havana. Judicial function was carried out by several courts. Unless a case could be appealed to the king himself, the highest court was the Council of the Indies at Madrid; the next highest court was the *audencia* of Havana. In the province itself, the highest judicial authority was the governor. He could select judges for special courts, either civil or military. Commandants of the districts were judges of limited jurisdiction. Beneath the commandants were the syndics or justices of the peace.[14]

In Baton Rouge the important official was the commandant of the post. Pedro Jose Favrot (1779–1781), Ignacio Delino de Chalmette (1781–1784), Francisco de Berges (1784–1787), and Jose Vesquez Vahamonde (1787–1795) served as commandants in that order. Although the last named was retired from the Spanish military in 1795 when the commandant of the District of Baton Rouge took over the post, he still continued to serve as acting commandant of the post when the commandant of the district was absent.[15]

The commandant had many duties. He had to see that the law was enforced and the peace preserved. It was his duty to examine all passports, and he allowed no one to settle in the district without permission of the governor. The commandant had jurisdiction over civil cases if the money involved did not exceed a certain amount. He could also punish slaves and arrest and imprison free persons for certain offenses. However, a transcript of all the evidence had to be sent to the governor. In more important cases, the commandant could

---

14. Chambers, *A History of Louisiana*, I, 302.
15. Miller, "The Spanish Commandant," 16.

take testimony and refer the case to the proper tribunal. He was also a notary who made inventories, kept records, settled estates, and issued reports. With all the formalities he had to observe, it was difficult for the commandant of the Post of Baton Rouge, or any other post, to exceed his authority.[16] As a rule, Spanish officials were very efficient administrators—at least on paper. Each official was responsible to the person immediately above him, and he had to justify practically everything he did in writing. This in itself was a curb both to irresponsibility and probably to initiative as well.

One of the most interesting of the cases to be judged during the administration of Commandant Favrot was the case of Marie Glass, a mulatto, who was tried for murder. This crime, in which a fifteen-year-old white girl was tortured to death, was committed in the District of Baton Rouge in 1779. Favrot worked closely with Judge Harry Alexander, a British judge, who submitted depositions from different people concerning the case. Reports were made in three languages—French, English, and Spanish. Favrot permitted the case to be tried before three British judges and three jurors. Marie Glass was found guilty of cruelly taking the life of the girl, and her husband was found guilty as an accomplice. When the sensational trial was finally over, the woman was sentenced to be "hanged by the neck" until dead. Her head was to be cut off and put on a pole at her place of residence and her hand nailed beneath the head. The trial and necessary reports took two months. At Favrot's request, the husband's sentence was commuted to life at hard labor. Acting Governor Piernas confirmed Marie Glass's death sentence in January, 1781. She was marched through the streets to the gallows and hanged on July 26, 1781. In commenting on

16. Martin, *The History of Louisiana*, 212.

Conquered by Spain 51

the case in his diary, Dunbar wrote, "On thursday last we held a Court at the fort for the Tryal [*sic*] of Molly Glass for the murder of a white girl [Emilia] & brought her in guilty, sentencing her to have her hand cut off & afterwards hanged until she is dead—This Tryal was made agreeable to the English laws under the Capitulation of Baton Rouge 21st Sept. last/"[17]

One of the most interesting aspects of Spanish legal documents of that period in Baton Rouge was the use of three languages. Just as in the Marie Glass case in 1779, English, French, and Spanish were used in legal documents up to the end of the Spanish period. Often all three languages were used in dealing with the same case. The petition might be in the language of the petitioner, but the official document might be in Spanish. Spanish governors apparently made every effort to be fair to their subjects even though this could be very difficult when they did not speak the same language.

Propagation of the Catholic faith was very important to Spanish conquerors of the Floridas. The language barrier was one of the obstacles the Spanish priest had to surmount. As a concession to the English-speaking populace (although a Protestant Englishman or American might have doubted this), the king requested that Irish priests be sent to Louisiana "in order to bring over the inhabitants and their families to the Catholic faith by the mildness and persuasion it recommends." Gayarré states that the priests arrived in 1787, but the church historian Roger Baudier said that they sailed from Spain in February, 1792. Confusion arises from the fact that more than one group of Irish priests came to Louisiana. Of

17. "Trial of Mary Glass for Murder, 1780," *Louisiana Historical Quarterly*, VI (October, 1923), 591–93, 642–43. Her place of residence was Brown's Cliffs, and, according to a copy of an old map in possession of the writer, this was located north of Baton Rouge; Eron Rowland, *Life, Letters, and Papers of William Dunbar*, 72.

the six who came to Louisiana in 1792, at least three served the people of Baton Rouge.[18]

Father Cirillo de Barcelona, who had served as chaplain of the Spanish forces under Gálvez when they captured West Florida, was made a bishop in 1782. West Florida was in his jurisdiction, and he was interested in establishing a church in Baton Rouge.

About 1790 two new ecclesiastical parishes were established, one of which was Baton Rouge. This step came rather late: first, because there is no record that French priests served Baton Rouge after 1722; and second, because during the British occupation of Baton Rouge nothing was done in the way of religious development. No doubt Anglican chaplains, who came with British military forces, held Protestant services at this time, but apparently they did not proselytize. Roman Catholics were free to practice their own religion in the British Province of West Florida. According to Roger Baudier, Catholics at Baton Rouge may have been served by Capuchin fathers at Pointe Coupee, especially since the church at Pointe Coupee had been in existence since 1738. There are records of baptisms at Pointe Coupee as early as 1728. It is also possible that the Baton Rouge post may have been served by priests from St. Gabriel, since that parish had been established about 1765. In any event, there does not seem to have been a separate parish with a designated pastor in Baton Rouge until 1792.[19]

There is no known record as to when the first church in

18. Gayarré, *History of Louisiana*, III, 178, 181; Martin, *The History of Louisiana*, 245; Baudier, *The Catholic Church in Louisiana*, 237, 241–42.

19. Baudier, *The Catholic Church in Louisiana*, 200, 204–207, 220. Cirillo was actually an auxiliary bishop, but in effect he served as bishop of Louisiana. Elisabeth Joan Doyle, *A Guide to Archival Materials Held by the Catholic Diocese of Baton Rouge* (Baton Rouge: Department of History and Archives of the Catholic Diocese, 1964), 35, 59.

Baton Rouge was built, but it must have been prior to 1792, because a church was there when the first resident pastor arrived. This was Father Charles Burke, an English-speaking Irish priest who served the Spanish king and was loyal to the point of signing his baptismal name as Carlos. Fortunately, he kept orderly records—also written in Spanish. The first official act to be recorded at Baton Rouge was a marriage on January 15, 1793, uniting Don Antonio de Gras and Genevieve Dulat. Interestingly, the bridegroom had donated the land on which the church was built, and it was called the Church of the Virgin of Sorrows—a sad name for a church in which Don Antonio and Donna Genevieve took their marriage vows. But later, in a petition granted in 1804, the name was apparently changed to the Church of Our Lady of Sorrows. The chapel served the town of Baton Rouge until a second church, built under the leadership of Father Antoine Blanc, was dedicated in honor of Saint Joseph on December 19, 1830.[20]

Father Charles Burke served as the first pastor for six and a half years, signing his last official entry in July, 1799. Besides performing his priestly duties, he served as the official interpreter for Spanish officials who needed someone proficient in the English language. Baton Rouge had no pastor for nine months after Father Burke's departure; then Father Francis Lennan of the order of the Capuchin fathers came to officiate, but it was not until April 27, 1800, that he signed as "Pastor of this Post." He probably remained in Baton Rouge until 1802, when one finds that Father Patrick Lonergan signed the records as "Pastor pro tem." Then Father Lennan served again, though he was by that time pastor of

20. Gassler, *History of St. Joseph's Church*, 7–9, 13–18, 35. Baudier, *The Catholic Church in Louisiana*, 220.

St. John the Baptist Church on the German Coast. Father Paul de St. Pierre also served the Baton Rouge church for a brief period. The Church of the Virgin of Sorrows does not appear to have had a permanent pastor from June, 1802, until May, 1803.

Baton Rouge was a relatively cosmopolitan little town at this time, because three great nations of Europe had left a cultural imprint that is evident even in the twentieth century. During the Spanish period, a citizen needed to be trilingual to be really effective. Father St. Pierre was apparently more than adequate. In Spanish, he signed his name Pablo de San Pedro; in French, Paul de St. Pierre; in Latin, Paulus Sancti Petri; and in German, his own native tongue, it was Paulus Heiligestein! Thoroughly confusing are his church records, which give every version except the German.

Father John Brady became the next resident pastor. His name appears for the first time in May, 1803. Possibly he came reluctantly, for he signed his records as one "temporarily performing the pastoral duties of the place," and he did this for sixteen years. He was given a special book left by Father Lennan when he died; and this book, written in Spanish, contained a record of mixed or non-Catholic marriages covering the years from 1794 to 1805. Father Brady remained in Baton Rouge for many years, and one finds that he sued the trustees of the church in 1824 for back salary due him by the church in Baton Rouge.[21]

Although the residents of Baton Rouge differed in national origin and were often disturbed by events far removed from their village, seeming almost to be at the mercy of foreign diplomacy, the planters still led a relatively pleasant life. And the plantation economy provided money and leisure

21. Gassler, *History of St. Joseph's Church*, 15–19, 29.

for important social gatherings for the more well to do. The town, high on a bluff above the floodwaters of the Mississippi, was surrounded by plantations where the art of gracious living was a matter of everyday life. Besides a great deal of informal visiting back and forth among neighbors, there was a certain formality connected with official entertaining of the commandant of the post or the governor of the district. Spanish officials had, no doubt, been influenced by the royal courts of Europe. Although the government was Spanish, the governor of the district was French, and most of the residents were British or American.

The main source of income was agriculture, though there was considerable trade and there were a few local industries. William Dunbar, a Scotsman who had received a land grant near Baton Rouge during the British period, and who later settled on a plantation south of Natchez, had experimented with indigo. Although he continued to grow indigo, he found the manufacture of staves for the West India market to be much more profitable. Generally, cotton and corn were, by far the most important crops.[22] Besides these basic products, planters raised vegetables and fruits and a wide variety of livestock—cattle, horses, sheep, and fowl.

Since cotton and corn could be laid by in late summer, master and slave alike had several weeks of leisure before harvest. Thus there was a period of partying and visiting before cotton-picking time. Mount Pleasant, a prosperous but not large plantation, was a good example of this kind of living. The master owned only six slaves and eighty-seven head of livestock, but the mistress used tablecloths and owned candelabra, three dozen dinner plates, and two dozen

---

22. Dunbar Rowland, *History of Mississippi*, I, 296. "Archives of the Spanish Government of West Florida," IV, 50, 191, 252.

cups and saucers. Some of the furniture was walnut and cherry. These are evidences of a genteel way of life and of the importance of social activities.[23] There were many larger plantations with numerous slaves. The owner of Montesanto plantation, Fulwar Skipwith, just above Baton Rouge, drove into town "from his palatial residence in the country in a splendid coach [and] four, with outriders and lackeys to match." Adam Boyd's estate could boast of having on hand "10,000 pounds of cotton in the seed picked by three negroes."[24]

Spanish records show that the women of Baton Rouge played an important role in plantation society. The West Florida Archives for this period cite many instances where women took legal action or made sales of property. They were also permitted to witness legal documents. Although she may have lived on a frontier, when the lady of the house went shopping in Baton Rouge, she could purchase beautiful materials—wool, silk, linen, and dainty lawn and muslins woven from cotton. Ribbons, lace edgings, and thread of both silk and cotton were also available. Fine hosiery, handkerchiefs, gloves, slippers, fans, hats, and powder for her hair were sold in the stores. Stationery, books, and fine imported wines helped to make living more pleasant. Besides the usual groceries, sugar, spices, coffee, and tea were available.[25] The wife of a wealthy cotton planter could buy locally most of the luxuries she desired.

By 1800 the professions and trades were well represented

23. *Ibid.*, XI, 3, 7.

24. James A. Padgett, "The West Florida Revolution of 1810, as Told in the Letters of John Rhea, Fulwar Skipwith, Reuben Kemper and Others," *Louisiana Historical Quarterly*, XXI (January, 1938), 6.

25. "Archives of the Spanish Government of West Florida," XII, 37, XIII, 146–55, I, 62.

in Baton Rouge. Besides many civil and military personnel, there were doctors, lawyers, a priest, interpreter, merchants and surveyors, as well as tailors, carpenters, masons, tanners, butchers, blacksmiths, bakers, and gunsmiths.[26] Even the slave trader was important.

Education was private, but teachers did not seem to fare so well. In 1806 "one school master jumped his board bill" at Baton Rouge, and his property was sold to satisfy his creditors. In 1805 another schoolmaster, Joseph Sharp, was killed by an angry parent, William Flanegan, as Sharp visited Peter Lawrence at his plantation. The murderer fled across the line into Mississippi, beyond the reach of Spanish law, and his property was seized by Spanish authorities.[27]

Although planters could hire private tutors for their children, no provision was made for educating the less fortunate. Many settlers were illiterate, and their children grew up with no education. During the Spanish regime Baton Rouge offered no public education. Manuel Gayoso de Lemos, who later governed Louisiana from 1797 to 1799, stated in 1792 that the only public school in Louisiana was in New Orleans, and he expressed a desire that more schools be established. In a letter to the king of Spain, Gayoso stated that education could solve some of the problems of the province, and he made a special request for "three (schools) in the jurisdiction of the government under my charge; it would have advantageous results, for not only would they form the hearts of children but would fill with gratitude those of their parents."[28]

26. *Ibid.*, XI, 332, XII, 394, XVIII, 253.
27. *Ibid.*, XI, 182A, X, 182.
28. James Alexander Robertson, *Louisiana Under the Rule of Spain, France, and the United States, 1785–1807* (Cleveland: Arthur H. Clark Co., 1911), I, 288–89.

Gayoso did not get his schools, but one may wonder what it might have meant to Baton Rouge if he had, since he owned a thousand acres of land near the Fort of Baton Rouge.[29] Contrary to Gayoso's thinking as to the advantages of education, Spanish schools could well have been a point of contention, since children of English-speaking parents would probably have been required to speak Spanish.

In the District of Baton Rouge, the plantation system, of course, was based on the institution of slavery. Although slaves were very valuable no doubt many were subjected to abuse in a system which degraded both master and slave. William Dunbar wrote about a "conspiracy" that took place in July, 1776. Some of his slaves were involved, and he wrote, "Judge my surprise! of what avail is kindness & good usage when rewarded by such ingratitude; 'tis true indeed they were kept under due subordination & obliged to do their duty in respect to plantation work, but two of the three had always behaved so well that they had never once received a stroke of the whip." He mentioned other instances when slaves ran away. Also, on one occasion he disclosed, "Mr. Ross set out for Orleans, sent Daphne with him, having given her, her freedom."[30]

Free men of color could and did own slaves in this district. One black, Jean Baptiste Marsie, freed his slave, a mulatto girl named Claire. She was a native of Louisiana and had been acquired from Armand Duplantier. Marsie gave her "full liberty now and forever." Carlos de Grand Pré notarized the document on March 13, 1807. There were also Indian slaves in the District of Baton Rouge as late as 1787.[31]

29. Holmes, *Gayoso*, 268.
30. Eron Rowland, *Life, Letters and Papers of William Dunbar*, 26–29, 46.
31. "Archives of the Spanish Government of West Florida," XII, 27, I, 73.

The Spanish government had a very generous land policy. Unlike the British policy, which required grantees to pay a tax on their land, the Spanish granted land freely and without charge. However, landholders were supposed to keep up roads, levees, bridges, and ferries. In 1789 Governor Esteban Rodriguez Miró specified that a grant six acres wide (fronting on a waterway) and forty acres deep could be granted to a family. The amount of land could be increased according to the number of persons in the family or according to the number of slaves owned; thus the acreage could be increased up to twenty acres across and forty deep. Grants were also made in proportion to the ability of the grantee to develop his land.[32]

During the Spanish regime, property in and near Baton Rouge became valuable, and several large tracts were subdivided. Captain Elias Beauregard developed one such subdivision. His plantation was the usual forty arpents, extending about one and one-half miles from the Mississippi River. He subdivided that portion between North and South boulevards and between East Boulevard and the river. Each lot was sixty by one hundred twenty feet; this area was known as Beauregard's Village. (It is now often called Beauregard Town.) Elias Beauregard sold no less than eleven lots in this subdivision during the month of July, 1807.

Edith Smith Devall subdivided the area from First to Ninth streets, taking in what is now Laurel, Main, and Florida streets. This section was called Devall Town. After 1794 a number of Islenos or Canary Islanders came to live in

32. Davis, *Louisiana: A Narrative History*, 138. Power to grant land communicated to the U.S. Senate, January 20, 1821 in *American State Papers. Public Lands*, III (Washington, D.C.: Gales and Seaton, 1834), 401, 433.

Baton Rouge. They settled on Spanish Town Road (now Boyd Avenue).[33]

One of the reasons land in Baton Rouge became valuable was its elevation above the flood level of the Mississippi River. A spring flood was a yearly occurrence, but in some years the devastation was greater than in others. In the spring of 1788 the river went on a rampage, and the flood was much worse than usual. It inundated all the lowlands around Baton Rouge and elsewhere in the district. Among those who suffered most were the Acadians who had settled Manchac just south of Baton Rouge. Governor Miró was able, through a special fund, "to succor them with corn and rice."[34]

In the 1790s residents of Baton Rouge became involved in a much more complicated problem than a natural disaster such as a flood. Frenchmen in Louisiana were emotionally involved in the politics of the French Revolution, and practically every ship from France brought agitators who kept them informed about conditions there. The Revolution, with its slogans about liberty, equality, and fraternity, was the most important topic of conversation, and Frenchmen "made little effort to conceal their opinions." In January, 1793, Louis XVI of France was beheaded. Spain declared war on France, and many Frenchmen in Louisiana naturally sided with their kinsmen in the mother country.[35]

Strangely enough, support for the Spanish monarch came from English-speaking settlers in Natchez and Baton Rouge. Even though allegiance to the Spanish crown had been forced

33. "Archives of the Spanish Government of West Florida," XIII, 73, 77–78, 106, XII, 59.

34. Caroline Maud Burson, *The Stewardship of Don Esteban Miró, 1782–1792* (New Orleans: American Printing Co., Ltd., 1940), 266–67.

35. Ernest R. Liljegren, "Jacobinism in Spanish Louisiana, 1792–1797," *Louisiana Historical Quarterly*, XXII (January, 1939), 50; Martin, *The History of Louisiana*, 259.

on them, and though they had little love for Spain, they cared even less for the French revolutionaries. Anglo-American settlers in Baton Rouge had been Tory and Loyalist during the American Revolution, and after the war, many Americans from the seaboard colonies fled to the haven of West Florida.[36] The militia at Baton Rouge could be counted on to support the king—definitely the lesser of two evils.

Recognizing a potentially dangerous situation that could result in an insurrection, the Baron de Carondelet (governor of Louisiana, 1791–1797) accelerated military preparations and began to drill supplemental forces. When an uprising did take place in Natchitoches, Carondelet chose Antonio Argote, captain of the militia at Baton Rouge, to take his forces and put down the insurrection. On January 13, 1796, Captain Argote successfully put an end to the rebellion and arrested the leaders, but he released them immediately and allowed them to return to their homes. His policy of conciliation was so effective that within a few days the inhabitants were shouting "Viva el Rey." Captain Argote remained in Natchitoches until the end of February, when he was ordered back to Baton Rouge.[37]

Preceding the trouble at Natchitoches, another frightening incident occurred near Baton Rouge. In April, 1795, a conspiracy, which was probably instigated by white revolutionaries, was uncovered at Pointe Coupee. Blacks of the area, who outnumbered whites, had planned to stage an uprising and massacre their masters. Black leaders were caught and punished, and the threatened outbreak by the slaves was avoided. About the same time, there was a rumor of a revolt at Baton Rouge which may have been a part of the same plot.

36. Liljegren, "Jacobinism in Spanish Louisiana," 79.
37. *Ibid.*, 50, 75–76.

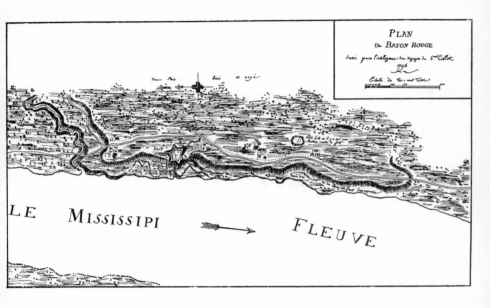

Plan of Baton Rouge, 1796. (Copy in Louisiana State Library)

The prompt action at Pointe Coupee may have prevented further trouble.[38]

Although Baton Rouge was increasing in population (1,513 by 1803) and was militarily important to the Spanish, Spanish commandants had let the fort deteriorate. On July 21, 1787, Jose Vesquez Vahamonde, commandant of the Post of Baton Rouge, awarded a contract to William Dunbar to furnish lumber needed to repair Fort San Carlos.[39] Apparently, no repairs of lasting significance were made because Carondelet wrote the king in 1794: "The Forts of Manchac and Baton Rouge are in ruins. Only the buildings have been repaired since they were conquered from the English [1779].

38. *Ibid.*, 63; Holmes, *Gayoso*, 171.
39. Martin, *The History of Louisiana*, 300; Miller, "The Spanish Commandant," 16.

Baton Rouge offers the most beautiful and advantageous location to dominate the river and to hold the enemy a sufficient time."[40] He added that its location was important to keep enemy forces from penetrating to New Orleans. Carondelet also suggested that Manchac be abandoned. This was accomplished the same year, and the commandant at Baton Rouge assumed control of Fort Bute when that command was merged with the command at Fort San Carlos.[41]

English-speaking settlers in Baton Rouge were willing to support Spanish authorities in certain crises, such as a slave revolt or a French uprising in Natchitoches, but there was a strong undercurrent of dissatisfaction because of basic differences in the Anglo-Saxon and Latin temperaments. It was also difficult to reconcile different approaches to religion and government. Protestants resented the fact that only the Catholic religion could be practiced in public. As to government—Englishmen openly took the required oath to serve the king of Spain, but there were secret reservations. They yearned for a representative form of government as practiced by American and English citizens. With their heritage, it was probably impossible for Anglo-Saxon West Floridians to be really loyal Spanish subjects.

However, there was a way out of this situation—they could leave. In instances where British subjects had indicated that they wished to leave the territory, Spanish officials had been indulgent in extending the time needed to dispose of property, collect and pay debts, and make the necessary arrangements to move. In 1786 the king issued a royal order declaring that permission would be granted to inhabitants to stay in Baton Rouge if they took the oath of allegiance to the

40. Robertson, *Louisiana Under the Rule of Spain*, I, 306–307.
41. Miller, "The Spanish Commandant," 56.

Spanish Crown and if they promised that they would not move out of the District of Baton Rouge without permission of the governor. Those who chose not to take the oath were ordered to leave, and the Spanish government offered to pay their transportation. The king was reimbursed by sale of property belonging to the deportees.[42]

Spanish officials were faced with another major problem—the influx of American pioneers. Esteban Miró (Spanish governor of Louisiana, 1785–1791) was assigned the impossible task of preventing Americans from gaining a foothold in West Florida. American traders who often came down the Mississippi River in flatboats, after seeing the mildness of the climate and the lushness of the land, went back to get their families. They made this land their home, and these new settlers brought with them the unmanageableness and independence of the American frontiersmen. Most of the Americans were Anglo-Saxon and Protestant, and they felt a kinship with the English in West Florida who, though more civilized and accustomed to a more gracious way of life, also had a streak of independence that resisted Spanish authority. This resistance provided common ground for the two groups and, eventually, resulted in rebellion against the Spanish government.

One historian wrote that "from the time he received his commission until he resigned, worn out and no doubt discouraged, Miró was continually striving to beat back the American advance guard." But it was like trying to hold back the waters of the Mississippi. In spite of Spanish restraints, a census taken in 1788 showed that the population of Baton Rouge had increased to 682—more than twice the 1785 count. Pointe Coupee, across the river, had more than 2,000;

42. Martin, *The History of Louisiana*, 245.

Feliciana, to the north, had 730 and Manchac had a populationof 284. Blacks outnumbered whites at this time.[43] These figures indicate that not just Baton Rouge but the whole area was increasing in population. Americans who became Spanish citizens were a crafty lot and were probably quite willing to give lip service to the Spanish monarch. Many of them, no doubt, intended to make every effort to unite with the United States at the first opportunity. To these frontiersmen the Spanish were foreigners who had no business here anyway—or so they rationalized. One can sympathize with Governor Miró (and with the Spanish commandant in Baton Rouge) who had to try to govern this polyglot population—American, English, Scotch, Irish, German, Spanish, French, Acadian, Indian, Negro, and related mixtures.

Soon Americans were aided in their push south by the Treaty of San Lorenzo which was signed by Spain and the United States in 1795. According to the provisions of this treaty, the southern boundary of Mississippi was acknowledged to be the thirty-first parallel, the Mississippi River was declared open to all the citizens of the United States, and the right of deposit at New Orleans was guaranteed for three years.[44]

Recognizing the boundary line to the south as the thirty-first parallel immediately increased the military importance of Baton Rouge, even though it would take a few more years for Americans to ease the very reluctant Spanish out of Fort Panmure in Natchez. Gayoso, the Spanish governor of the Natchez District, had no real supervision over the Post of

43. Albert Phelps, *Louisiana: A Record of Expansion* (Boston: Houghton Mifflin Co., 1905), 153–54; Gayarré, *History of Louisiana*, III, 170, 215.
44. Davis, *Louisiana: A Narrative History*, 127–28.

Baton Rouge, but Governor Carondelet had frequently made him responsible for its defense. Thus Gayoso was in a position to know that the evacuation of Natchez would make it extremely important that adequate defenses be prepared along the new boundary line. Gayoso also felt that Baton Rouge should be made the most important military post in lower Louisiana, not only because it would be the one nearest the American frontier at that point but also because it had easy access to Mobile and Pensacola by way of Manchac through the Iberville and Pearl rivers and through Lakes Pontchartrain, Borgne, and Maurepas. Gayoso wanted to build a line of blockhouses, five leagues apart, along the frontier dividing the District of Baton Rouge from American territory. He wanted a strong post in Feliciana with a commandant in residence and at least a hundred troops. This became especially important when, in the spring of 1798, Spanish troops were finally evacuated from Natchez and from other Spanish posts in American territory.[45]

Jose Vasquez Vahamonde was the last commandant of the Post of Baton Rouge. After 1795 the governor of the District of Baton Rouge was also the commandant of the post. In 1803, when Baton Rouge became the capital of the Province of West Florida, the governor of the Province assumed command. This arrangement continued until 1810.[46]

Carlos de Grand Pré, still governor of the District of Baton Rouge in 1795, had been appointed by Gálvez after the capture of Baton Rouge in 1779. Though he was French by birth, he had served the Spanish king well and was very popular with the people of the district. Vincente Folch, governor

45. Holmes, *Gayoso*, 166, 232, 237–38.
46. Miller, "The Spanish Commandant," 57.

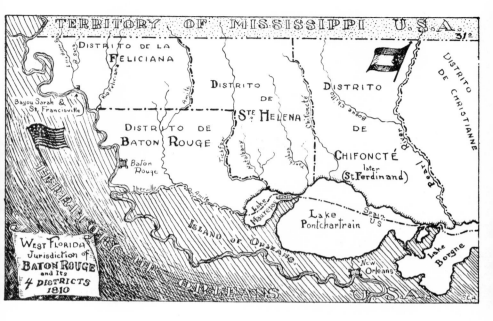

Spanish West Florida

of the Floridas, disliked and distrusted Grand Pré.[47] Eventually, he would see him replaced, and Grand Pré's successor would lose Baton Rouge for the Spanish.

Baton Rouge had failed as a settlement under the French; it had begun to flourish under the British; and it continued to make progress during the Spanish regime. Plantations and farms lined the Mississippi River and the village of Baton Rouge had grown to be a small but thriving town. According to a population count in 1805, it numbered 3,820 people.[48]

47. Gayarré, *History of Louisiana*, IV, 69–70.
48. Davis, *Louisiana: A Narrative History*, 142; Baton Rouge *Morning Advocate*, October 14, 1965.

IV

Expansionism
and Revolution

BY 1800 the little Spanish Post of Baton Rouge, in the District of Baton Rouge and the Province of West Florida, was composed of a blend of influences from France, England, Spain, and the United States. Baton Rouge had been a pawn in the chessmanship of three great European powers for over a quarter of a century and, between 1800 and 1810, was again about to become a point of contention. But by then a new player was in the game; and, strangely enough, although the most unimportant of the four, this young, inexperienced, but very clever and slightly unscrupulous contestant would win.

The new but very intuitive nation with the "smallest of armies, without conscription," and "with a minimum of naval forces" would out-maneuver the most skillful players in Europe.[1] A brash new nation, beset by the growing pains of the very young and puffed up by a previous victory, felt a need to reach out to new frontiers; and it was canny enough to wait until the great powers were busy fighting each other before it would make a move. President Thomas Jefferson gave specific verbal expression to this idea in 1803, when he said: "We have some claims . . . to go eastwardly [into West

1. Samuel Flagg Bemis, *A Diplomatic History of the United States* (Rev. ed.; New York: Henry Holt and Co., 1942), 215.

Florida]. . . . These claims will be a subject of negotiation with Spain, and if, as soon as she is at war, we push them strongly with one hand, holding out a price in the other, we shall certainly obtain the Floridas, and all in good time."[2]

Jefferson spoke of "negotiation" and "price," but neither was really necessary. It was just a matter of time until Americans on the frontier would take over. A good frontiersman learned to take advantage of situations for the sake of survival—like a good horse trader, he had no regrets when he got the best of a bargain. Outsmarting a rival was more a matter of necessity than of conscience. Spanish West Florida simply could not exist with an American frontier to the north and to the south. A developing national spirit could express itself only in expansion. "The normal and inexorable push of the American pioneers was not to be denied. It was Spain's misfortune . . . to be in their way." As the seaboard became crowded, free men moved west; by 1785 some fifty thousand had crossed the Alleghenies to the rich valley beyond. Perhaps the first manifestation of aggressive expansionism was in the conniving of Americans to obtain West Florida. It was in fact "invoked in spirit, in word and deed, by American statesmen from Jefferson" on.[3]

Why was West Florida—so small on a great continent— important to powerful rulers in Europe? The answer was concerned with the right of navigation of the Mississippi River, because whoever controlled West Florida maintained some control over the use of this vitally important waterway. Even a century before, when Bienville turned a British ship

2. Bailey, *A Diplomatic History of the American People*, 164.
3. Bemis, *A Diplomatic History of the United States*, 215; Bailey, *A Diplomatic History of the American People*, 175.

back and headed it downriver to the Gulf because Louisiana
had been claimed for the French monarch, it was possible to
see the genesis of a controversy over navigation of the river.
Thus arose the very important "Mississippi Question" which
was, eventually, to lead to the purchase of Louisiana.[4]

Another reason for the importance of West Florida was its
control of seaports on the Gulf of Mexico—especially Mobile
and Pensacola. Casa Yrujo, Spanish Minister to the United
States, wrote: "The ports of Florida . . . would make it easy
for us to annoy greatly the American commerce in case of
war, and would in like degree furnish the Americans, if the
Americans should possess them, the same means of annoying
ours, and of carrying on an immense contraband trade from
them, especially from Pensacola and Mobile, with our prov-
inces in the Gulf of Mexico."[5] Florida was situated "like a
giant pistol, with the peninsula serving as the butt and West
Florida the barrel," and this barrel was "pointed directly
at the mouth of the all-important Mississippi River." Most
of the southern boundary was on the Gulf Coast. Aware of
the strategic and commercial value of West Florida, Robert
Livingston, United States Minister to France, would have
been content with that territory alone since this would mean
control of part of the eastern bank of the river and also the
shores of Mobile Bay. If New Orleans were unattainable, a

4. Davis, *Louisiana: A Narrative History*, 41; Jean-Baptiste Bénard de la Harpe, *The Historical Journal of the Settlement of the French in Louisiana* (Lafayette: University of South-western Louisiana, 1971), 24–26. In 1699, on a trip down the Mississippi, Bienville encountered an English frigate in a bend of the river. The ship's captain was very unsure as to where he was, so Bienville told him he was in French territory, and the English captain turned and went down the river. The place has since been called *Detour des Anglais* or English Turn. The English had an eye on the Mississippi even then. Robert Livingston, *The Original Letters of Robert R. Livingston, 1801–1803* (New Orleans: Louisiana Historical Society, 1953), 1–2.

5. Henry Adams, *History of the United States* (New York: Charles Scribner's Sons, 1898), II, 252.

channel to the Gulf by way of Manchac and the Iberville River would provide the necessary outlet.[6]

In the Treaty of Paris, 1763, France had ceded to Great Britain the east bank of the Mississippi except for the Isle of Orleans and had also granted equal rights of navigation. But Spain, after obtaining this territory by conquest in 1779, was in position to determine who could navigate the river. By the Treaty of San Lorenzo, 1795, Spain granted the right of the United States to navigate the Mississippi from its source to the Gulf and the right of deposit at New Orleans for three years. In 1802 Juan Ventura Morales, intendent of Louisiana, on orders from his government, revoked the right of deposit, and the controversy was resumed.[7]

President Jefferson argued that when Great Britain yielded the Floridas to Spain, she did not yield a privilege which belonged to the United States—use of a waterway that was guaranteed by natural rights. He insisted that one nation could not deny to another the right of navigation and that "inhabitants on the upper course of a river had the right to pass in and out of its mouth." He cited rivers in Spain which flowed through Portugal. In addition to natural rights, American population on the Mississippi River and its tributaries was greater than the population of the Spanish in the same area. Jefferson also cited Roman law to prove that navigation was a public privilege and must of necessity include the right of deposit. These arguments sounded impressive, but the only practical solution was for the United States to somehow obtain land bordering the Mississippi River and

6. Bailey, *A Diplomatic History of the American People*, 163–64; Isaac Joslin Cox, *The West Florida Controversy, 1798–1803* (Gloucester, Mass.: Peter Smith, 1967), 74. This is a reprint of a 1918 edition published by Johns Hopkins Press.

7. Cox, *The West Florida Controversy*, 74.

thus put a stop to power plays in which England, France, and Spain were constantly involved.

When rumors of a retrocession of Louisiana to France by Spain became commonplace, they were of worldwide importance. For Napoleon to be empire building in the Mississippi Valley was a prospect which disturbed the British as much as it did the United States. Rufus King, United States Minister to England, wrote as much to Secretary of State Madison in June, 1801.[8]

The transfer was of immediate concern to the people of Baton Rouge who might be faced with problems of citizenship and property rights. Pedro Favrot, first commandant of the Post of Baton Rouge, exemplified this status. He had returned in 1801 with the understanding that he would be in command when Grand Pré was promoted. He was ordered, instead, to serve as commandant of the Post of the Plaquemines. On hearing of the retrocession of Louisiana to France, Favrot asked for two years' leave of absence with the intention of selling his property, collecting debts owed him, and making any changes that would protect his interests after the transfer. The King granted him leave, which began on the day of the transfer of Louisiana to France. Although the Spanish assured him that Baton Rouge would not be affected by the transfer, Favrot went to his plantation on the west side of the river. When he was told he would forfeit his leave if he did not return to Spanish territory, he replied that he could not return and asked to be retired after more than forty-two years of service. A French Creole, who served Louis XV as Pierre Joseph de Favrot and Carlos III and Carlos IV of Spain

8. *Ibid.*, 27–28; Rufus King to James Madison, June, 1801, in *American State Papers, Foreign Relations*, II (Washington, D.C.: Gales and Seaton, 1832), 509.

as Don Pedro Jose Favrot, he would now become an American citizen and serve a new country.[9]

For a French Creole, the transfer of allegiance from one Latin monarch to another might not have been too difficult, but to Anglo-Saxon Americans, schooled in independence and democratic processes, the idea of a Napoleonic Louisiana was frightening. When word of the probable retrocession reached Washington, President Jefferson, who had always been pro-French, became apprehensive. Once more the right of navigation of the Mississippi River was in jeopardy, or might be if Napoleon came to power in the Mississippi Valley and refused to recognize treaties made previously with Spain. Charles Pinckney, United States minister to Spain, tried to negotiate. First, he tried to persuade the Spanish government to guarantee the United States rights of navigation of the Mississippi if Spain did cede Louisiana to France; next, he was authorized to tempt the Spanish with a guarantee of their colonies west of the river if they would cede the Floridas to the United States. Pinckney was unsuccessful. In the meantime, Napoleon Bonaparte was also trying to trade the Duchy of Parma in Europe for the Floridas, but he was told that the Spanish king was unwilling to sacrifice any more territory in America. Bonaparte was incensed, and it may have been at this point that he decided to make the boundaries of the Louisiana Purchase so nebulous.[10] If he could not obtain the Floridas, he would make it more difficult for Spain to keep them.

Robert Livingston arrived in Paris in December, 1801,

9. Helen Parkhurst, "Don Pedro Favrot, a Creole Pepys," *Louisiana Historical Quarterly*, XXVII (July, 1945), 679–734.

10. Cox, *The West Florida Controversy*, 66–69, 72.

with orders to discuss the right of free navigation of the Mississippi River and the right of deposit in case Louisiana had been retroceded to France. He was also authorized to purchase West Florida and the Isle of Orleans if the retrocession were irrevocable. The French had failed when they tried to get both the Floridas and Louisiana; but now they experienced some success when Spain delivered to France "the colony and province of Louisiana" in the secret Treaty of San Ildefonso on October 1, 1800. The French also failed when they tried to exchange the two Floridas for the Duchy of Parma, and the Floridas remained in the possession of Spain. Livingston knew this because he wrote to Secretary of State James Madison, "Florida is not, as I told you before, included in the cession." Livingston knew, also, that Pinckney in Spain had the same assurance, for he wrote to Madison that "by letter I just received from Mr. Pinckney, he still supposes the Floridas are not included and had made a proposition [to Spain] to buy them."[11] There seems no doubt that all parties involved understood this to be true before the Louisiana Purchase. The Treaty of San Ildefonso took place in 1800 and the Louisiana Purchase in 1803.

Concerning the Louisiana Purchase, Thomas A. Bailey has written: "Livingston and Monroe had fruitlessly tried to buy West Florida. . . . They knew perfectly well they had failed to do so when they signed the purchase treaty." It was after the date of the purchase that representatives of the United States began wishfully assuming that the Floridas had been purchased along with Louisiana. The French had been pur-

---

11. Livingston, *Original Letters of Robert R. Livingston*, 21; Francis P. Burns, "West Florida and the Louisiana Purchase," *Louisiana Historical Quarterly*, XV (July, 1932), 397–99; Robert Livingston to James Madison, September 1, 1802, in *American State Papers, Foreign Relations*, II, 516, 526.

posely obscure concerning the boundary, and when quizzed, their representative answered, "I can give you no directions; you have made a noble bargain for yourselves, and I suppose you will make the most of it."[12] The Americans did just that.

When the United States Congress legislated for the new territory in 1804, West Florida was considered a part of the Louisiana Purchase. In the first session of the Eighth Congress, when an act setting up a territorial government was passed, it included the land "south of the Mississippi Territory," which surely included the District of Baton Rouge in the Province of West Florida.[13] However, this was only on paper; the Spanish did not choose to withdraw from West Florida, and Jefferson preferred not to use force. Juan Manuel de Salcedo, the last Spanish governor of Louisiana, was determined to remain as governor of West Florida, which, he said, was "that part of Louisiana which still remained to us." Salcedo pointed out the commercial and agricultural advantages of the region and suggested that Baton Rouge be fortified because of "its strategic importance as a point from which to threaten New Orleans." But those in charge recalled that Baton Rouge was practically surrounded by hostile Americans who might utilize any excuse to move in. Vizente Folch was appointed governor of West Florida, and Pensacola became his headquarters; Baton Rouge, though not the capital of the province, was destined to become its storm center.[14]

12. Bailey, *A Diplomatic History of the American People*, 164; Burns, "West Florida and the Louisiana Purchase," XV, 403; Davis, *Louisiana: A Narrative History*, 161

13. "An Act Providing for Temporary Government of the Territory of Orleans," March, 1804, in *Annals of the Congress of the United States* (Washington, D.C.: Gales and Seaton, 1852), 8th Cong., 1st Sess., 1803–1805, p. 1038.

14. Cox, *The West Florida Controversy*, 149–50.

During the hectic days following the Louisiana Purchase, many residents of Baton Rouge, particularly those of American or British extraction, felt a keen sense of disappointment at not becoming a part of the United States. Grand Pré, commandant of the Post of Baton Rouge, pursued a cautious policy in dealing with the disaffected residents. Some "showed their dissatisfaction by insolent threats against the local officials or by open disobedience." Not only were Spanish officials plagued by problems within the district but also by difficulties created by agitators in American territory. The lawlessness of brigands from the hill country north of the district posed a definite threat to law-abiding citizens. And no authority seemed to be able to control these outlaws. Grand Pré wrote Robert Williams, governor of the Territory of Mississippi, that "disorder, confusion, violations, outrages, plunder, insult to the magistrates and attempts on the flag" had taken place. From such incidents the West Florida Revolution arose. Cooperation was essential between Spanish and American officials, yet it was not forthcoming. When William Flanegan (the angry parent) murdered John Sharp (the schoolmaster) and fled into the Mississippi Territory, it was a foregone conclusion that Spanish soldiers who went to search for him would not be successful.[15]

Revolt was in the air. At Bayou Sara, the Kemper brothers, Nathan, Reuben, and Sam, fighting sons of a Baptist preacher, were the first to take decisive action. They hated everything Spanish and proposed to strike a blow for "Floridian Freedom." According to Dunbar Rowland, "the Kemper affair was the beginning of the disorder that finally

15. *Ibid.*, 151; Frederick W. Williamson and George T. Goodman (eds.), *Eastern Louisiana* (Shreveport, La.: The Historical Record Association, 1939), II, 485–86; *American State Papers, Foreign Relations*, III, 685–87.

furnished some actual warrant" for the Americans to take possession of West Florida.[16]

Sam and Nathan Kemper had already been in trouble with Spanish authorities and had been driven from West Florida into Mississippi. When it appeared that more trouble was brewing, Grand Pré sent out a patrol, under Captain Vizente Pentado, to guard the Mississippi-West Florida boundary.

On August 7, 1804, the Kempers invaded West Florida withan armed group of about thirty men. Marching to Bayou Sara, they seized Captain Pentado and burned his house and cotton gin; then they began the march to Baton Rouge. Their objective was to take over the fort and seize the governor.[17]

This attempt to overthrow the Spanish government was accompanied by a Proclamation of Independence supposedly written by Edmund Randolph of Pinckneyville. It stated: "For a people to be free it is sufficient that they will it. Whereas, the depotism under which we have long groaned, has grown into an insupportable burthen, and as it is long since admitted men were born with equal rights, we the undersigned inhabitants of that part of the (Spanish) dominions called West Florida, have resolved to throw off the galling yoke of tyranny and become freemen, by declaring ourselves a free and independent people, and by supporting with our lives and property that declaration."[18]

Published in the Charleston *Courier*, September 2, 1804, the proclamation proposed that when the West Floridians attained emancipation, they would offer themselves to "some

16. Stanley C. Arthur, *The Story of the Kemper Brothers*, reprinted from the St. Francisville *Democrat*, n.d., 3; St. Francisville *Democrat*, July 8, 15, 22, 29, 1933; Dunbar Rowland, *History of Mississippi*, I, 410.
17. Arthur, *The Story of the Kemper Brothers*, 4–5; Cox, *The West Florida Controversy*, 155–56.
18. Cox, *The West Florida Controversy*, 155–56.

government accustomed to freedom." No doubt, the government they had in mind was that of the United States. The insurgents marched under a banner of seven blue and white stripes with two stars on a field of blue.[19]

Warned in advance of the impending attack, Governor Grand Pré summoned the militia and prepared to defend Fort San Carlos. Rumors estimated the approaching force at 200 men, but actually the insurgents numbered about 30. Nathan and Sam Kemper had planned to take the Spanish by surprise, but when they reached the fort on August 8, Grand Pré's militia was waiting, and a few shots were exchanged. At noon Kemper offered to exchange the prisoners they had taken at Bayou Sara for prisoners held by the Spanish. Grand Pré refused. The next day, August 9, the discouraged revolutionaries retreated to Bayou Sara where they tried to set up headquarters and continue the revolt. Grand Pré organized an armed force of 150 volunteers—most of them from the Amite and Comite River areas. Commanded by Armand Duplantier, they pursued the insurgents, who simply "faded into the magnolia forests" of the Mississippi Territory. Protected by officials of the American government, who refused to turn them over to Spanish authorities, the rebellious West Floridians remained free to continue their activities.[20]

Governor Folch, on hearing news of the revolt, made plans to go to Baton Rouge with reinforcements, but he hesitated long enough to send men ahead to build a military road from Mobile. He and his men left Pensacola on August 31, and upon arriving at Baton Rouge, found everything quiet. The

19. *Ibid*.
20. Arthur, *The Story of the Kemper Brothers*, 7; Cox, *The West Florida Controversy*, 158.

governor made a few suggestions for defense of the fort and returned to Pensacola.[21]

Governor Claiborne of Louisiana wrote President Jefferson, "I find Kemper's Riot, for it cannot fairly be called an insurrection, is viewed northward as an important affair." He also wrote Secretary of State James Madison, "the expedition of Governor Folch to Baton Rouge was certainly unnecessary. Kemper's insurrection, as it is called, was in fact nothing more than a riot."[22] Claiborne played down the situation, but the revolt foreshadowed the West Florida rebellion of 1810.

Hardly had residents of Baton Rouge settled down, when rumors of a conspiracy involving Aaron Burr, former vice-president of the United States and notorious political schemer, began to be circulated widely. Baton Rougeans were especially jittery because Baton Rouge was said to be an important military objective in this alleged conspiracy to build an empire in the West. When Burr passed through West Florida in 1805, Burr's movements were followed with care by Spanish officials, but he "afforded them no occasion to apprehend him." The following year, in July, Burr wrote his famous letter to General James Wilkinson, commanding general of the United States Army, stating that his forces would be ready by November. Burr planned to move down the river, join Wilkinson at Natchez, and then go down the river and capture Baton Rouge.[23]

21. Cox, *The West Florida Controversy*, 161–62.

22. William C. C. Claiborne to Thomas Jefferson, October, 1804, in Clarence Edwin Carter (ed.), *The Territory of Orleans, 1803–1812*, Vol. IX of *The Territorial Papers of the United States* (Washington, D.C.: Government Printing Office, 1940), 314–15; William C. C. Claiborne to James Madison, April 21, 1805, in Carter (ed.), *Territory of Orleans*, 437–38.

23. Cox, *The West Florida Controversy*, 188–90; Phelps, *Louisiana: A Record of Expansion*, 234.

In September, 1806, Governor Folch at Pensacola was informed that Burr might soon attempt to take over West Florida; and at Baton Rouge, Grand Pré was determined to put up a good defense "although he had only sixty men, one-half of them invalided, and an uncertain militia largely composed of Americans." As usual, the fort at Baton Rouge was in poor condition, and in reality it was merely a "holding point surrounded by a hostile population." According to Isaac J. Cox, Baton Rouge was populated with "four or five" thousand people, most of whom were of Anglo-Saxon extraction. Further, the Baton Rouge area was more productive agriculturally than other areas in West Florida; but, Cox adds, "It was so enclosed by neighboring American territory as to be defenseless."[24]

In the autumn of 1806 there were rumors that thousands of Kentuckians and soldiers would come down the Mississippi the following spring. This force would be joined by the Louisiana militia and "liberated slaves" for an attack on Baton Rouge. Folch, distrusting Grand Pré, went to Baton Rouge with reinforcements, and returned to Mobile when the danger of attack had passed.[25]

Another complication occurred when Governor Claiborne informed Governor Folch that he (Claiborne) had been ordered by the United States government to cut off all communication with West Florida and to blockade Bayou Manchac. Such a blockade would seriously interfere with exporting cotton from Baton Rouge. Even more important, perhaps, it would prevent Folch from sending reinforcements to Baton Rouge in case of attack.[26] This embargo, plus re-

24. Cox, *The West Florida Controversy*, 191–93, 212.
25. *Ibid.*, 202–206.
26. *Ibid.*, 219–21. The embargo went into effect in January, 1808. According to Folch, the Americans were going to try to "starve the Spaniards out of West Florida."

peated violations of Spanish territory by Americans, made continued friendly relations impossible.

After the Burr fiasco, Major John Ellis, an American officer, remarked that Grand Pré was incompetent, the government that he represented extremely weak, and the fort at Baton Rouge a tempting object of attack. Then in July, 1808, Grand Pré unwittingly entertained a French agent, General Octaviano Davilmar, who was on a mission for Napoleon to the Spanish colonies. When the agent was arrested in Texas and the report of his visit to Grand Pré made public, the governor of the District of Baton Rouge was ordered to Havana to explain.[27]

To the people of Baton Rouge, the recall of Grand Pré was a disaster. He had been a mild governor and had been responsible, at least in part, for the peace and prosperity of the district. Petitions went out for his reinstatement. One addressed to Grand Pré stated: "In all the time of your rule, you have exerted yourself to perceive our wants. You have heard our petitions. Every individual always found free access to you and you never refused to listen to the general voice or to individual representations which were for the public good or to remedy some evil."[28] Grand Pré had served the Spanish government from 1779 until 1809. In many instances, loyalty to the Spanish government by the people of Baton Rouge was more a personal loyalty to Grand Pré than to Spain. When it was rumored that he would be replaced, the murmurings of Anglo-Americans became more ominous.

Early in December, 1808, Thomas Lilley, a syndic, or justice of the peace, wrote Grand Pré concerning the discontent and unrest of the citizens of the Baton Rouge District.

27. *Ibid.*, 312–14.
28. *Ibid.*, 314–15.

Lilley requested that the syndics and alcaldes be permitted to meet and discuss methods of quieting the people. Grand Pré consented, and within a few days they met at Thompson's Creek in the Feliciana District. Besides petitioning Spanish officials to defer Grand Pré's recall, they asked that he be allowed to stay until the new commandant could become accustomed to the people. They also offered to help finance the government (which was a very revolutionary idea); and then they called for another meeting on December 23, 1808. This put Grand Pré in a difficult situation, because such activity would never be approved by Spanish authorities in Havana. However, he agreed to the meeting. When the meeting took place and the men learned that Grand Pré really did not approve, they adjourned immediately. These first meetings were undertaken in the name of Ferdinand VII, but the most casual observer could detect a revolutionary trend. In 1809 Grand Pré was finally sent to Havana to face charges of pro-French activities. In the summer of the same year, Pedro Favrot, lifelong friend and executor of Grand Pré's estate, learned that Grand Pré "had died of a broken heart before he could be tried for disloyalty."[29]

Don Carlos de Hault de Lassus succeeded Don Carlos de Grand Pré as governor of the District of Baton Rouge. The new governor had an easygoing, vacillating personality and was surely not the best choice to govern a turbulent, discontented people. He exercised poor judgment in his choice of subordinates to help administer the government. He also resented the affection West Floridians felt for Grand Pré and their obvious regret at his departure for Havana.[30]

29. *Ibid.*, 314–24; Stanley C. Arthur, *The Story of the West Florida Rebellion* (St. Francisville, La.: St. Francisville *Democrat*, 1935), 29, 30.

30. Cox, *The West Florida Controversy*, 333–34.

Resentment against de Lassus seemed to be greatest in the area around Bayou Sara, upriver from Baton Rouge. The people complained of corruption in government, saying that their "government officials [were] open to bribery." Most of the complaints were general, but one specific charge against Raphael Crocker, the governor's secretary, accused him of bribery. Crocker maintained that the charge was inspired by the Americans, and his fellow officials dismissed it. Law enforcement had become so lax and officials so corrupt that the planters' complaints fell on deaf ears.[31]

In the Feliciana district, which included Bayou Sara, Thomas Estevan was the military commandant and Father Francisco Lennan was curate. Neither was popular, and between "the cross and the crown" citizens were being bled for services of all kinds. The planters of Feliciana felt that what they really needed was a well-organized local government, but in Spanish West Florida such thoughts bordered on treason. Any plans the planters made would have to be in secret to escape a traitor's death or at best a life in prison.[32]

Prominent citizens, in spite of the danger, began to hold secret meetings in Feliciana at Troy plantation, the home of John Hunter Johnson. Estevan warned de Lassus, who sent two trusted English-speaking messengers from Baton Rouge to talk with the dissident citizens. George Mather and Philip Hickey met with the planters and sent word back to de Lassus that there was nothing to fear from these meetings.[33]

While this was going on in Feliciana, two Frenchmen from New Orleans were holding nightly meetings in the vicinity of Baton Rouge "under the pretext of defending

31. *Ibid.*; Arthur, *The Story of the West Florida Rebellion*, 30.
32. Arthur, *The Story of the West Florida Rebellion*, 31.
33. *Ibid.*, 32–35.

themselves from Spanish plots." Diego Morphy, vice-consul at New Orleans, warned de Lassus that the French were planning revolution in West Florida. De Lassus gave the malcontents three days to get out of the district. He may have been too severe since some of the Frenchmen involved had lived in Baton Rouge a long time. They had taken an oath of allegiance to the king of Spain and had served in the militia.[34]

American officials observed with pleasure the growing disaffection in Baton Rouge. William Barrow, a wealthy Bayou Sara planter, wrote to a friend in Nashville that the existing government in West Florida was "quite done." His friend sent a copy of the letter to President Madison. Governor Holmes of Mississippi also wrote a letter on June 20, 1810, in which he said that complete anarchy prevailed in West Florida and that regular officials had ceased to function effectively. The people were divided and uncertain, but they were afraid to involve themselves in a premature revolt even though a majority desired annexation to the United States. Holmes added that he did not expect any foreign power to intervene "with the possible exception of Great Britain."[35] Under these circumstances, any Spanish governor of West Florida could hardly have been successful.

The American government was playing a waiting game. Jefferson had said, "We shall certainly obtain the Floridas and all in good time." The time was drawing noticeably nearer, and the broad wings of the American eagle hovered, ever closer, over its prey; surely by June, 1810, its talons were visible even to de Lassus.

On Saturday, June 23, over five hundred people gathered

34. *Ibid.*, 33; Cox, *The West Florida Controversy*, 335–36.
35. Cox, *The West Florida Controversy*, 338–39, 329.

at Egypt plantation in Feliciana to take steps to "secure themselves against foreign invasion and domestic disturbances." The leaders introduced a prearranged plan by which the Province of West Florida could be governed. A council, made up of representatives from the various districts, would be given general powers of government. Spanish officials could remain in their positions if they complied with the terms set down by the council. This plan was adopted by voice vote with only eleven dissenting. They then proceeded to elect representatives from Feliciana: John Hunter Johnson, William Barrow, John Mills, and John Rhea. These men would ask the other districts to elect representatives to serve on the council.[36]

News of the Feliciana meetings spread quickly to the other districts, and on July 6, 1810, leading citizens of Baton Rouge petitioned the governor for permission to call a similar meeting. The petition was signed by Philip Hickey, George Mather, Joseph Sharp, Samuel Fulton, Fulwar Skipwith, Dr. Andrew Steele, Thomas Lilley, John Davenport, George and William Herries, Philemon Thomas, John Morgan, and Edmund Hawes. Governor de Lassus consented, stating that since the purpose of the meeting was to "insure the tranquility and well-being of every citizen in the jurisdiction" he would gladly grant permission for meetings in Baton Rouge, St. Helena, and Chifoncte (Tangipahoa). He even sanctioned the meeting that had already taken place in Feliciana.[37]

On July 25 representatives of the people assembled in Convention at St. John's Plains in Feliciana to organize a government to "promote the safety, honor, and happiness of

36. Arthur, *The Story of the West Florida Rebellion*, 37; Cox, *The West Florida Controversy*, 340–41.
37. Arthur, *The Story of the West Florida Rebellion*, 38–39; Cox, *The West Florida Controversy*, 348–49.

our beloved King Ferdinand VII." Representatives elected to the convention by the various districts were: from Feliciana, William Barrow, John Johnson, John Mills and John Rhea; from Baton Rouge, Philip Hickey, Thomas Lilley, Manuel López, Edmund Hawes, and John Morgan; from St. Helena, Joseph Thomas, John W. Leonard, William Spiller and Benjamin O. Williams; from Tangipahoa, William Cooper.

Members of the convention proceeded to pass a resolution which defined its general powers: "Resolved, That this Convention created by the whole body of the people of the government of Baton Rouge, and by the previous consent of the governor, is therefore legally constituted to act in all cases of national concern which relate to this province, to provide for the public safety, to create a revenue, and with the consent of the Governor, to create tribunals civil and criminal."[38] Then the elected representatives of the people of West Florida prepared a list of grievances against the Spanish government. A committee was also appointed to work on a plan for "redressing these grievances and for defense of the province." Having thanked the governor for his cooperation, they wished him a long life, and they adjourned until August.[39]

To the next meeting, which took place on August 13, 1810, the governor of Mississippi sent his personal representative, Colonel Joshua G. Baker. This meeting lasted three days, and it was apparent that the representatives were marking time. They could not finish writing the ordinance, so they adjourned until August 22. On this date they met at

38. Arthur, *The Story of the West Florida Rebellion*, 49; Cox, *The West Florida Controversy*, 348–49.

39. Arthur, *The Story of the West Florida Rebellion*, 50–53; Cox, *The West Florida Controversy*, 349–50.

Baton Rouge and passed an ordinance "providing for the Public Safety, and for the Better Administration of Justice within the Jurisdiction of Baton-Rouge, in West-Florida." The document was signed by Carlos de Hault de Lassus as governor and John Rhea as president. It was also signed by the representatives. The meeting was adjourned on August 29. A committee of three had been appointed to act with the governor on administrative matters until the representatives reconvened on the first Monday in November.[40]

Although the governor appeared to acquiesce in the convention's plans to strip him of all real authority, he was secretly stalling for time and hoping for help from Pensacola in answer to an appeal he had sent in July. Governor Holmes, after his observer at the convention had reported, wrote to Robert Smith in Washington that de Lassus had divested himself of practically all his power, retaining little but the "name and salary." Holmes added, however, that "surrender of his authority was not a matter of choice on his part." But now the time for delaying tactics had arrived and de Lassus refused to consent to the appointment of certain officials—specifically Fulwar Skipwith as judge and Philemon Thomas as brigadier general. De Lassus also pointed out that certain other matters must have the approval of his captain general in Havana. His apparent acquiescence had ended.[41]

This stiffening of his attitude toward the insurrectionists may have been due in part to a visit by Captain Luis Piernas, a Spanish army officer, who came to Baton Rouge in September. He had been sent by Governor Folch with six thousand pesos to pay the soldiers. After several conferences with de

40. Arthur, *The Story of the West Florida Rebellion*, 58–86; Cox, *The West Florida Controversy*, 363–82.

41. Arthur, *The Story of the West Florida Rebellion*, 93–96; Cox, *The West Florida Controversy*, 381–83.

Lassus, Piernas left for Pensacola with a letter from de Lassus to Folch explaining the situation in Baton Rouge. Piernas also carried a letter from William Cooper at Tangipahoa, dated September 12, 1810, in which Cooper assured the governor that at the next meeting the delegates to the convention would finish the work they had begun and would overthrow the last vestiges of Spanish rule. However, when Captain Piernas arrived in Pensacola in October it was already too late for Folch to send reinforcements to de Lassus.[42]

On September 20 de Lassus gave a dinner to celebrate the "peace and harmony" that existed between his government and the people. He ordered a twenty-one-gun salute to commemorate this friendship. Stanley C. Arthur wrote that Philemon Thomas, who attended the dinner, smiled knowingly, his blue eyes gleaming. Two could play at this game. That morning one of Thomas' men had intercepted a message meant for Governor Folch in Pensacola. De Lassus had sent this latest message to Shepherd Brown of St. Helena who would forward it to Folch. In the letter de Lassus asked for reinforcements to quell the insurrection at Baton Rouge, saying that he was virtually a prisoner of the rebels.[43]

Philemon Thomas, on receipt of the message, had informed Philip Hickey of the situation. Hickey volunteered to be the Paul Revere of the West Florida rebellion. He rode quickly to spread the news, and at the Plains in Feliciana he was joined by other riders. On September 21 six of the leaders met at Troy plantation. They knew they could all be hanged for treason if they did not move quickly. Once more riders were dispatched to gather arms and men for the im-

42. Arthur, *The Story of the West Florida Rebellion*, 99; Cox, *The West Florida Controversy*, 382–87.

43. Arthur, *The Story of the West Florida Rebellion*, 100–101; Cox, *The West Florida Controversy*, 394–95.

Philemon Thomas. (From the collection of
the Louisiana State Museum)

pending attack and to notify the representatives that the convention would be in session the next day.[44]

The convention assembled, on the special order of President John Rhea, in St. Francisville, on the bluff above Bayou Sara. Present at the meeting were John Rhea, John H. Johnson, William Barrow, John Mills, Philip Hickey, and Thomas Lilley.[45] This day, September 22, 1810, was a very important and very busy day for the delegates. Even though the revolutionaries thought that Governor Folch might be on his way with reinforcements, they took time out to assemble the convention and proceed with the business of authorizing a revolution.

One of the purposes of the assembly was to consider the behavior of His Excellency Charles de Hault de Lassus. In addition to his duplicity in sending for troops while he pretended to cooperate with the convention, he had now balked at delivering a copy of the ordinance with his signature. The convention decided that "this Convention in the name of the good people of the Jurisdiction of Baton Rouge declare that the said Charles Dehault Delassus [sic] is unworthy of their confidence, and ought no longer be entrusted with the administration of the Laws as the first magistrate of a people whom he has insulted and betrayed."[46]

Then the governor was divested of all authority, and it was agreed that his powers would be exercised by the convention. The commandant of the militia would enforce the laws and "insure public tranquility." The convention directed that the commandant of the militia, Philemon Thomas,

44. Arthur, The Story of the West Florida Rebellion, 101–102; Cox, The West Florida Controversy, 394–95.
45. James A. Padgett (ed.), "Official Records of the West Florida Revolution and the Republic," Louisiana Historical Quarterly, XXI (July, 1938), 716.
46. Ibid.

would also take possession of the garrison at Baton Rouge as soon as possible.[47]

President John Rhea also informed Governor Holmes of the situation and asked for any help the Mississippi governor could give. Rhea wrote that they had been "abandoned and betrayed" by de Lassus and that Folch was beyond all doubt marching toward Baton Rouge. Then the convention adjourned to "meet at the town of Baton Rouge on Tuesday next the 25th."[48]

On the same day that these events were taking place in St. Francisville, Baton Rouge seemed very quiet—at least on the surface. But an undercurrent of rebellion ran strong and deep. The amiable governor, who had secretly sent for troops from Pensacola, spent the morning at the home of Philip Hickey—the same Philip Hickey who had secretly warned plantation owners that the governor had sent for troops to put down the insurrection. The governor still did not know that his messenger had been intercepted on September 20— on the same day that the governor had entertained representatives of the convention and had fired the twenty-one-gun salute in celebration of their harmony.[49] Residents of Baton Rouge had learned well the art of deception from their European masters.

De Lassus might well have used this time to repair the fort. Fort San Carlos at Baton Rouge was in a run-down condition, and though de Lassus had been advised by subordinates to repair it, the governor had made no attempt to do so. The stockade, which was the chief defense, had gaps, and it was through one of these openings that the insurgents were able

47. *Ibid.*
48. *Ibid.*, 718–19.
49. Arthur, *The Story of the West Florida Rebellion*, 100–101; Cox, *The West Florida Controversy*, 395.

to slip into the enclosure around the fort before the guards could sound an alarm. De Lassus had complained that gunpowder was short, but he had plenty with which to salute American gunboats as they went up and down the river and enough to fire a twenty-one-gun salute in celebration of "harmony" that existed between the governor and the leaders of the convention. According to Isaac Cox, there were twenty cannons in good condition. With such weapons, a competent commander could have stopped the pitifully small force that captured Fort San Carlos.[50]

The Spanish garrison at Baton Rouge was manned with regular army troops aided by civilian militia. The militia, many of whom were Americans, lived off the compound but could be ordered into action if the need arose. Not all the officers and men were assigned to duty in the fort. For example, Estevan and three soldiers were on duty at Bayou Sara until just before the capture of Fort San Carlos. Others were on duty at the hospital. One soldier had been cutting wood for Captain Crocker and rarely performed military duties while he worked for the captain. On the morning of the attack, there were twenty-eight officers and men assigned to duty, including Lieutenants Louis de Grand Pré and Juan Metzinger, the only commissioned officers within the enclosure. The rest were sleeping in the village.[51]

If the Spanish defenders of the fort were unprepared, it certainly was not due to a lack of warnings. On Thursday, Commandant Thomas Estevan had been forced to leave St. Francisville with his men. The priest, Father Francisco Lennan, accompanied them. This alone should have been an

50. Cox, *The West Florida Controversy*, 389–90.
51. *Ibid.*, 393–96.

indication that trouble was brewing. And then on Saturday, September 22, no fewer than three warnings were delivered to de Lassus telling that the fort would probably be attacked. Lieutenant Francisco Morejon, an officer at the fort, reported that in the morning a messenger came with word that the people of Feliciana were arming and planning an attack. Between four and five in the afternoon another messenger from John Murdock at Bayou Sara warned that there would be an attack. The last messenger came at one o'clock on the morning of the twenty-third. This time Murdock sent word that the attack would come before dawn.[52]

Apparently the third warning was heeded, for the governor was awakened, and he went to the fort. Subordinates reported later that the governor only came to secure a guard for his own house and that he took no extra precautions at the fort. Louis de Grand Pré, though he did not believe there would be an attack, began to assemble members of the regular army and those of the militia so they would be ready if the need arose.[53]

Outside the town, a handful of rebels were gathering for the attack. Since there were only about seventy-five men in the entire force, they hoped to take the Spanish by surprise. In a conference to determine the best approach, Larry Moore, a Kentuckian, suggested that the cavalry could slip into the fort by following a cow path. (Milk cows entered the fort through a gap in the cypress palisades on the side facing the river.) The horses were led down to the river so the cavalry could approach the fort from that direction. Stanley C. Arthur wrote:

52. *Ibid.* Arthur, *The Story of the West Florida Rebellion*, 103–105; Cox, *The West Florida Controversy*, 393–95.
53. Cox, *The West Florida Controversy*, 396–98.

In single file the horsemen urged their mounts up the steep river bluff and threaded their mounts through the herd of milk cows; the cow path was distinct in spite of the thickening fog that hung close to the surface of the wide Mississippi, for the day was about to break. The opening in the cypress palisades was found just as Larry Moore had predictd and so quietly did the horsemen make their way into the fort that they were lined up on the edge of the parade ground before the sentry [could sound the alarm].[54]

The horsemen advanced to the blockhouse and Grand Pré gave the command to fire. The rebels returned the fire and after a brief skirmish the battle was over. By this time, the rest of the force had entered the gate. The Spanish soldiers were demoralized as much by the method of warfare as by the battle itself.[55]

The next day, September 24, 1810, Colonel Philemon Thomas reported to the convention:

Sir: In obedience to the order of the Convention bearing date the 22d Inst. I directed Major Johnson to assemble such of the Cavalry as might be ready at hand, and march immediately for the fort of Baton Rouge. I then proceeded to Springfield where I found forty-four of the Grenadier company, commanded by Colonel Ballenger waiting the orders of the Convention. At one o'clock on the morning of the 23d. we joined Major Johnson and Captain Griffith with 21 of the Bayou Sarah Cavalry.[56]

Thomas added that "five or six other patriotic gentlemen" joined this force. At four o'clock they advanced on the fort with orders not to fire until they were fired upon. The Spanish wre ordered to surrender, but according to Thomas, they answered with a "discharge of musket fire from the guard-

54. Arthur, *The Story of the West Florida Rebellion*, 104–105, 110.
55. *Ibid.*, 107.
56. Padgett, "Official Records of the West Florida Rebellion," 719–20.

house . . . which we briskly returned." The rebels suffered no casualties, but Lieutenant Grand Pré and a private were killed and four more were wounded. The rebels took twenty-one prisoners including de Lassus. In his report Thomas had high praise for his men. He said, "the firmness and moderation of the volunteers who made the attack was fully equal to that of the best disciplined troops.[57]

Thus a handful of men, with the moral support of Americans, unseated the power of Spain in West Florida. That this was inevitable was apparent to Spanish officials. Although the loss of life was small, even this seemed unnecessary. More than one writer surmised that Grand Pré gave the order to fire as a reckless effort to vindicate the family name. Isaac Cox wrote that "Grand Pré had given the order to fire and his fate was only what every soldier must expect."[58]

When Governor de Lassus put in a belated appearance, he found that his men were being made prisoners by the rebel forces. Ordered to give up his sword, he refused; then a Feliciana volunteer knocked him down with the butt of his gun and was about to "run the bayonet through him" when Philemon Thomas intervened. Another Bayou Sara resident fired a pistol so close to the governor's head that "the power of Spain in the jurisdiction of Baton Rouge near swooned from fright."[59]

Early that morning, it was called to the attention of Major Isaac Johnson that the red and yellow banner of Spain was still floating over the fort. It was quickly lowered, and Major Johnson attached "his flag to the halyards and a new ensign rose to the top of the staff." Wild cheers greeted the raising

57. *Ibid*.
58. Cox, *The West Florida Controversy*, 400.
59. Arthur, *The Story of the West Florida Rebellion*, 104–106.

The County of Feliciana, 1810

of the new flag—a single star on a field of blue. According to Stanley C. Arthur, the star was Masonic in character and represented the "five points of fellowship" under which the leaders of the rebellion had held their secret meetings.[60]

Amid cheers of "Hurrah for Washington," Major Johnson and his troops rode into the village—dragging the Spanish flag in the dust behind "the flying feet of Isaac Johnson's horse."[61] The victors this time were not as generous as their Spanish conqueror had been thirty-one years before when the English Fort New Richmond surrendered to Bernardo de Gálvez. Perhaps this was because the frontier was the real conqueror, and Philemon Thomas and his volunteers did not have centuries of tradition to show them the way. They were products of a vigorous new America that was on its way, and heaven help the weaker neighbor in its path. The conquest of West Florida was simply a beginning.

60. *Ibid.*, 107, 158.
61. *Ibid.*, 108.

V

Republic
to State

THE TASTE OF victory was sweet on that exciting September morning when the revolutionaries unfurled the flag of the Republic of West Florida. Annexation to the United States had long been the dream of most West Floridians, but there were many problems to be solved before West Florida could achieve statehood. The reality of that achievement would be, at least to some, a disillusioning process.

The immediate problem was how to deal with Spanish officials who might be in hiding. Some had been able to slip away during the confusion after the attack. The priest, Francisco Lennan, escaped to the home of Captain Celestino de Saint Maxent at Manchac and later was able to make his way to Pensacola. The Spanish governor's secretary, Rafael Crocker, "abandoned his commander, ran to the river bank, where finding a skiff, he crossed to the other side." Crocker's home was searched, and his wife complained that the searchers "harassed her" and confiscated their property. Francisco Morejon crossed the river and eventually reached New Orleans. Gilbert Leonard was arrested after four days, but was permitted to remain in his home. Spanish soldiers who had not been able to escape were imprisoned in the fort. Later, they were released and allowed to go to Pensacola. Members of the militia who were loyal to Spain were confined to their homes and their weapons confiscated. The governor, de

Lassus, was imprisoned. Released later by Fulwar Skipwith, he went to live in American territory.[1]

While those loyal to the Spanish government were trying to get as far away as possible, others were flocking to Baton Rouge. Colonel Hugh Davis of Homochitto reported that so many Mississippians had gone to support the "American cause" in Baton Rouge that their families had appealed to him for protection. Davis feared a black revolt might be caused by Spanish agitators, and he was afraid such a disturbance would spread to Mississippi. Governor Holmes of Mississippi sent troops to the West Florida-Mississippi border where order was "so thoroughly maintained that the Commanding Officer soon withdrew the patrol of regulars to Fort Adams."[2]

After the fort at Baton Rouge had been secured, an order was posted demanding that inhabitants of the town surrender their arms. Issued by Philemon Thomas at his headquarters in the "Fort of Baton Rouge [on] this 23d day of September 1810," the order required that all firearms and "other offensive weapons be surrendered immediately to Thomas. If they met this condition, the people of Baton Rouge would be allowed to "remain in quiet possession of their property: and would be protected in the "enjoyment of all privileges to which they may be entitled by the laws of the country and the ordinances of the Convention."[3]

The next order of business for Thomas was a written report to John Rhea, president of the Convention. In this report,

1. Arthur, *The Story of the West Florida Rebellion*, 109, 110; Cox, *The West Florida Controversy*, 404, 508; William C. C. Claiborne to Secretary of State Robert Smith, December 24, 1810, in W. C. C. Claiborne, *Official Letter Books of W. C. C. Claiborne, 1801–1816* (Jackson: Mississippi State Department of Archives and History, 1917), V, 59.

2. Cox, *The West Florida Controversy*, 406–407.

3. Arthur, *The Story of the West Florida Rebellion*, 109–110.

made on September 24 from the Fort of Baton Rouge, Thomas described in detail the capture of the fort.

On the following day the patriots of Baton Rouge also prepared a statement for the delegates to the Convention in which they declared their loyalty to that body. Addressed to the "Representatives of the free people of West Florida in Convention Assembled," the document declared that the people of Baton Rouge "are highly gratified" at the presence of this "honorable body" which is the "legitimate organ of a Sovereign people" and that they will recognize no other government unless it "derives authority" from the Convention.[4] The document then declares that "Peace is desirable to all on honorable and safe principles"; but they were goaded beyond endurance. The people had been "borne down by Subaltern Tyrants, Insulted and Betrayed; and an Infernal Machine at work to Rivet on us Eternal Chains—we flew to arms in obedience to your orders and we Trust your honorable body will never allow the sword to be sheathed till the work of Regeneration is complete, and rights, liberties, and properties of our citizens secured by a free Representative Government and Equal laws."[5]

But not everyone was loyal to the convention, nor was everyone completely happy about the success of the rebels at Baton Rouge. Those opposing the convention were gathering in St. Helena under the leadership of Shepherd Brown who was trying to organize a force to oppose convention forces. Aware of this opposition, Philemon Thomas took precautions at the fort, and "every man that could be spared from the plantations rallied at Baton Rouge to support the Convention." Eventually the force grew to between 500 and

4. *Ibid*.
5. *Ibid*.

600 men. It was later reduced to 104 soldiers under the command of Captain John Ballinger.[6]

It was evident that the convention would have to set up a government now that they were no longer governed by the Spanish. In all the excitement, it would be easy for civilians and soldiers alike to get out of hand. So at the first session, a temporary government was instituted by a proclamation "Done in Convention, at the town of Baton Rouge, on Wednesday the 26th day of September, in the year of our Lord one thousand eight hundred and ten."

The "Representatives of the people of West Florida" declared that they would soon secure for their constituents "the blessings of liberty and equal rights" on a permanent basis, but that until this could be done "the ordinances and resolutions adopted by the Convention, with the concurrence of the Governor, on the 22 day August last, are considered as law." There was one exception—the powers that had been vested in the governor would now be exercised by the convention.[7]

In this first assembly of the convention after the coup at Baton Rouge, delegates also declared that the Spanish governor's actions had absolved them of any allegiance to him and gave them the right to declare their independence. Writing to Governor Holmes of Mississippi, who seems to have been their own special agent, the delegates said: "We have been abandoned and betrayed by our Gov. Delassus [*sic*] who is now anxiously awaiting the arrival of Gov. Folch and avowedly with the determination of cooperating with him in any manner he may direct." The letter continued by saying the

6. Cox, *The West Florida Controversy*, 411; Arthur, *The Story of the West Florida Rebellion*, 123.
7. Arthur, *The Story of the West Florida Rebellion*, 112.

delegates were enclosing the proclamation just passed and promised that a Declaration of Independence would soon follow. The letter suggested that any militia put in motion under the pretext of "preserving the tranquility of your own Territory could not fail to favor our cause, it would give a check to the Spanish and animate the honest though timid Americans." It was suggested further that "if a gun battery could be prevailed upon to drop down to the neighborhood of Baton Rouge the Dons would be paralyzed."[8]

The proclamation and letter were sent immediately to the governor of Mississippi. It does not seem strange that a copy of the first official act would be forwarded to this particular governor. The insurgents apparently identified more closely with the English-American residents of Mississippi than with the French residents of the Territory of Orleans; yet, they preferred to be a part of the state of Louisiana when it was admitted to the union, perhaps because it was apparent that Louisiana would be admitted as a state first.

The next communication from the convention president, John Rhea, was a letter to the governor of Mississippi also dated September 26, 1810. Enclosed was the Declaration of Independence which the delegates asked Governor Holmes to forward to President Madison. The delegates stated that "the present Government and the people of this state" wanted to become an "integral and inalienable portion of the United States."[9] Holmes forwarded the letter and the declaration to Secretary of State Robert Smith.

The declaration, passed by the "Representatives of the

8. *Ibid.*, 112–13. Holmes had already sent troops to the West Florida–Mississippi boundary.
9. John Rhea to David Holmes, September 26, 1810, in *American State Papers, Foreign Relations* III (Washington: Gales and Seaton, 1832), 396.

people of West Florida, in Convention Assembled" stated
that the citizens of West Florida had been loyal to the Spanish
government as long as there was any hope of receiving protection for their property and lives. They had made certain
regulations "in concert" with the governor. The citizens of
West Florida had entered into a compact in good faith and
had been assured of the good faith and cooperation of the
governor. But the governor had encouraged, "in the most
perfidious manner, the violation of ordinances sanctioned
and established by himself as the law of the land. Being thus
left without any hope of protection from the mother country,
betrayed by a Magistrate whose duty it was to have provided
for the safety and tranquility of the people," the delegates
declared that it became their duty to provide for their own
security "as a free and independent State, absolved from all
allegiance to a Government which no longer protects us."
They continued, "We, therefore . . . declare the several
districts composing this Territory of West Florida to be a
Free and Independent State." They added that they had the
right to "institute for themselves such form of Government
as they may think conducive to their safety and happiness;
to form treaties; to establish commerce; to provide for their
common defense," and to perform in every way as a "free and
independent nation" and they called on all foreign nations to
respect the declaration and acknowledge their independence.
This document was signed by John Rhea, president, and
Andrew Steele, secretary, of the convention.[10]

Having sent a copy of the declaration to Governor Holmes
of Mississippi, the delegates then sent a second copy to Governor Claiborne of the Territory of Orleans with a letter asking that he, too, forward the declaration to the president.

10. *Ibid.*

Claiborne was in Washington at this time and, according to Stanley C. Arthur, did not reply, but Holmes replied within a week. In his reply, dated September 30, 1810, the governor of Mississippi assured John Rhea that he would lose no time "in forwarding these important documents to the President of the United States." He asked to be informed of any new developments and closed with "honor and great respect for you and your colleagues."[11]

Even though the convention was not in session, having adjourned until October 24, 1810, its competent president continued his efforts to communicate with the president of the United States. From Baton Rouge, on October 10, Rhea wrote to Secretary of State Smith. Through the secretary, he made a direct appeal to the president for his consideration of the following information: that in 1806, when the United States was authorized to purchase East Florida, France was asked to intercede with Spain to relinquish West Florida; that in all diplomatic correspondence, West Florida had been considered a part of the Louisiana Purchase; that the United States had legislated for West Florida though it deferred taking possession; that France would not complain if the United States recognized West Florida's independence because Napoleon had urged Spanish Americans to declare their independence; and that England would not complain because "this measure was necessary to save the country from falling into the hands of French exiles . . . and other partisans of Bonaparte, who are the eternal enemies of Great Britain."[12]

Rhea then asked that West Florida be admitted as a state or territory of the United States and that the people be per-

11. Arthur, *The Story of the West Florida Rebellion*, 114–15.

12. *Ibid.*, 124; John Rhea to Robert Smith, October 10, 1810, in *American State Papers, Foreign Relations*, III, 395–96.

mitted "to establish [their] own form of Government, or to be united with one of the neighboring territories, or a part of them in such a manner as to form a state." If the United States government thought it proper to attach West Florida to a territory, "the inhabitants of this commonwealth would prefer being annexed to the island of Orleans."[13]

He pleaded, also, that West Florida's claim to public lands not be contested since the United States had "tacitly acquiesced in the claim of France or Spain for seven years," and he added that the "people of this Commonwealth" had "wrested the government and the country from Spain at the risk of their lives and fortunes." Remembering, also, that many of the settlers in this area were people who had not fought against England during the Revolutionary War, he asked that deserters from the United States be given pardons and "exemption from further service in the army or navy of the United States." His last request was a familiar one—a loan of $100,000 to be paid back by the sale of public lands. He suggested that this could be more or less a secret agreement with the secretary of the Treasury.[14]

This letter indicates that Rhea, merchant, planter, alcalde for Feliciana under Spain, and now president of the convention, was an astute and able leader. He wanted West Florida to be a part of the United States, but he wanted to make sure that the people of West Florida were treated fairly. He was saying that they had fought their own battles while the United States stood on the sidelines in the seven years prior to 1810 and that now they deserved some consideration. However, he was bargaining with a government that con-

13. *Ibid.*
14. *Ibid.*

tinued to declare to the world that it had purchased West Florida in 1803. According to Isaac J. Cox, there would have been no problem in securing pardons for deserters, but the United States would never waive its right to public land.[15]

Secretary Smith replied, through Governor Holmes, that the United States government could not recognize "in the convention of West Florida any independent authority whatever to propose or to form a compact with the United States." Although the people of West Florida and Baton Rouge might disagree, the United States government could not admit that West Florida had not been purchased. Smith wrote that "the people of West Florida must not for a moment be misled by the expectation that the United States will surrender, for their exclusive profit, what had been purchased with the treasure and for the benefit of the whole."[16]

Yet, West Floridians were still fighting for this land that the United States had purchased; in October, Philemon Thomas marched toward St. Helena to put down an uprising. Michael Jones, a Tory who was still loyal to the Spanish king, surrendered his men to Thomas and signed the Declaration of Independence. Shepherd Brown also advised his men "to disperse and save themselves." Brown tried to escape, but was captured and imprisoned with his friend de Lassus at Baton Rouge. After Thomas was able to put down this attempt to overthrow the government at Baton Rouge, resistance practically ceased except for one attempt to "stir up a mutiny at Baton Rouge and free de Lassus. The Feliciana

15. Arthur, *The Story of the West Florida Rebellion*, 28; Cox, *The West Florida Controversy*, 417.
16. Robert Smith to David Holmes, November 15, 1810, in *American State Papers, Foreign Relations*, III, 398.

dragoons quickly quelled the mutineers and banished them from the province."[17]

The one freedom that residents of Baton Rouge had enjoyed under the Spanish king was freedom from taxation. This was a tangible freedom; and, as such, Spanish officials thought it would be more important than an intangible freedom, such as freedom of religion. Governor Folch at Pensacola had mistakenly assumed that when the people of Baton Rouge learned they would have to pay taxes under the new government they would gladly help him restore order there. Taking all of this into consideration, the convention met in Baton Rouge on October 5, 1810, to repeal some of the taxes that had been passed on August 22. The first resolution repealed the tax on slaves, and the second reduced taxes on all land by classing it according to quality. Since land values varied, some of the delegates felt that it was only fair that owners of the better lands should pay higher taxes.[18]

The convention received no official communication from President Madison before convening the October 24 session. The purpose of the session was to consider a report by a constitutional committee composed of John Hunter Johnson, Edmund Hawes, and John Leonard. The document they prepared was based on the Constitution of the United States and would go into effect in November. This constitution provided:

For a governor to be elected by a general assembly biennially, and the government of the republic to be divided into three branches: legislative, executive, and judicial. The legislature to consist of a senate and a house of representatives with the representatives to be

17. Cox, *The West Florida Controversy*, 411–12; Arthur, *The Story of the West Florida Rebellion*, 120, 121.

18. Arthur, *The Story of the West Florida Rebellion*, 109; Cox, *The West Florida Controversy*, 409.

chosen annually; and the senators triennially. The new state was divided into five districts—Baton Rouge, New Feliciana, St. Helena, St. Ferdinand and Mobile. Each district was entitled to one senator and three representatives, with the exception of Feliciana, which was allowed a single senator and four representatives.[19]

On October 26 the convention adopted the constitution. It would go into effect when the delegates met in November. After this action the delegates to the convention appeared to be stalling for time. Perhaps they still hoped to hear from the president of the United States. Again they appointed a committee to conduct the government: Philip Hickey and John Morgan of Baton Rouge, John H. Johnson, John Mills, and William Barrow of Feliciana. The committee selected St. Francisville as the capital, where the general assembly would meet "on the third Monday of November next" to choose a governor "on the second day after a quorum of both houses shall be formed."[20]

Officials of the government were not at all certain of the loyalty of French refugees, though they had been assured that French attachment to Bonaparte "was feigned, in order to worry the Spaniards." This may have been the reason Captain Ballinger was left guarding the fort at Baton Rouge. He was ordered "to keep safe all state prisoners, maintain discipline amongst the 115 soldiers . . . and cautioned to be on guard against any surprise attack." Ballinger was also advised to salute American gunboats going up and down the Mississippi River.[21] Fearing France, England and Spain, the new government thought it wise to be friendly with the United States. To some West Floridians it would become an ironic

19. Arthur, *The Story of the West Florida Rebellion*, 128.
20. *Ibid.*; Cox, *The West Florida Controversy*, 427–29.
21. Cox, *The West Florida Controversy*, 429; Arthur, *The Story of the West Florida Rebellion*, 427–28.

twist of fate that their nearest neighbor and the one most trusted would, by military force, take their beloved West Florida. It also seems incredible that a tiny piece of ground in the interior of a great continent should have been so important to the great powers of Europe. Perhaps it was simply that in losing West Florida, France, England, and Spain lost their last foothold in the Mississippi Valley and consequently all chance of colonizing west of the Mississippi River.

On Saturday, November 10, the people of West Florida elected senators and representatives, and on the appointed day the assembly convened with what must have been a feeling of apprehension that their deliberations would be of no lasting importance. However, with no official communication from President Madison and amid rumors of a military takeover by the United States Army, they proceeded with the business of the government. John W. Leonard was elected president pro tempore of the Senate, and Dudley L. Avery became Speaker of the House of Representatives. The assembly elected as governor Fulwar Skipwith of Baton Rouge.[22]

Having served the United States government as consul in Paris, Skipwith had come home to recover a fortune that had been reduced during his service abroad. Although he did not seek the position of governor of West Florida, there was every reason why he should have been chosen. He accepted the governorship "not from vanity, but because he hoped, with the aid of Dr. Andrew Steele and other patriots, to avoid anarchy and confusion until annexation could be consummated." Skipwith had supported the Declaration of Independence because he thought this was the best way for West Florida to become a part of the United States.[23]

22. Cox, *The West Florida Controversy*, 432.
23. *Ibid.*, 433.

In his inaugural address, the governor stated that the people of West Florida had a natural right to independence, but that "neither gain nor implied promise of protection led them to take this momentous step." Completely sincere in his attachment to the United States, Skipwith's ultimate aim was to see the Republic of West Florida annexed to that power. He said: "Where the voice of justice is and humanity can be heard, our declaration and our just rights will be respected. But the blood which flows in our veins like the tributary streams which form and sustain the father of rivers, encircling our delightful country, will return if not impeded to the heart of our parent country. The genius of Washington, the immortal founder of the liberties of America, stimulates that return, and would frown on our cause should we attempt to change its course."[24]

One could wish that, somehow, this loyal American's pride could have been spared in the events that followed. Skipwith did not object to the military occupation of Baton Rouge by the United States Army as such, but he did object to the lack of any official communication from Washington before the occupation. He felt that as governor of the Republic of West Florida, he should have been given more consideration. President Madison, on the other hand, could not communicate "officially" with a nonexistent governor of a nonexistent republic, because it was the position of the United States government that West Florida had been purchased by the United States in 1803, and the president did not need permission to move troops into American territory.

After his inauguration, Governor Skipwith found himself under pressure from Reuben Kemper and his cohorts in New Orleans to send an expedition to free all of West Florida.

24. *Ibid.*, 434.

Their first objective would be Mobile. Although Baton Rouge was the "political storm center of West Florida," Mobile had also experienced considerable agitation against the Spanish government. But because it was closer to Pensacola, the people of Mobile were of necessity a little more cautious.[25]

On November 28, 1810, a draft for the Mobile expedition was begun, and excited preparations for war took place. Fifty-five "Sons of Liberty" sang as they marched from Baton Rouge to join other recruits at John Stuart's plantation. Lieutenant Charles Johnson and only twenty-five men were left at the fort to protect Baton Rouge.[26]

Even if successful, the expedition would be futile because President Madison in Washington had already taken steps that would make the army and government of the West Florida Republic unnecessary. The president knew, perhaps better than any other official in Washington, that as long as Baton Rouge and Mobile remained under the jurisdiction of Spain, or any other power, that New Orleans was insecure. As secretary of state he had tried to obtain West Florida and, except for fear of war, would have seized Baton Rouge after 1803. Now the time was much more opportune, because during the years since 1803 Americans had poured into the District of Baton Rouge. These Americans would support any move made by President Madison. But the president knew also that he would be criticized by other governments. On October 19, 1810, he wrote Jefferson that "our occupancy of West Florida would be resented by Spain, by England and by France, and bring on, not a triangular, but a quadrangular contest." Knowing full well that Congress

25. *Ibid.*, 434–37.
26. *Ibid.*; Arthur, *The Story of the West Florida Rebellion*, 129.

would meet in five weeks, Madison decided to take matters into his own hands. On October 27, 1810, the president proclaimed that Governor Claiborne would take possession of West Florida as far as the Perdido River. This action would forestall foreign intervention and hasten the restoration of order to West Florida.[27]

The proclamation issued by Madison is interesting because, like its predecessor the Louisiana Purchase Agreement, it is a model of ambiguity. The president said that the territory between the Mississippi and the Perdido rivers had at all times been claimed by the United States as a part of the Louisiana Purchase "in the same extent that it had in the hands of Spain, and that it had when France originally possessed it."[28]

He continued by saying that the United States had refrained from taking possession not because they "distrusted their title" but because if they kept talking long enough, they would be successful in an "amicable negotiation with a just and friendly power." In other words, they would eventually obtain West Florida. Now that a crisis had come about in West Florida, it was necessary for the United States to take possession because "the tranquillity and security of adjoining Territories are endangered." Although they would take possession, "it will not cease to be a subject of fair and friendly negotiation and adjustment."[29]

William C. C. Claiborne was authorized to take possession and to exercise over West Florida the "authorities and functions legally appertaining to his office." The people were

27. Adams, *History of the United States*, V, 305–309; Arthur, *The Story of the West Florida Rebellion*, 130.

28. Proclamation by the President of the United States, October 27, 1810, in *American State Papers, Foreign Relations*, III, 397–98.

29. *Ibid.*

asked to respect the governor, to obey the laws, to maintain order, and to cherish harmony with the assurance that they would be protected "in the enjoyment of their liberty, property and religion."[30]

On the same day that the proclamation was issued, Secretary of State Smith wrote Claiborne to proceed to Mississippi Territory. After he arrived at Natchez, copies of the proclamation would be printed in English, Spanish, and French and be distributed throughout the region. Claiborne would then proceed to Washington, Mississippi, and make arrangements with Governor Holmes and the commander of the regular army troops for military assistance before taking possession of West Florida.[31]

It was December 1, 1810, by the time Claiborne could reach Washington, capital of the Territory of Mississippi. He and Holmes believed that "a great majority of the inhabitants of the District of Baton Rouge would receive with pleasure the American authorities." But they knew, also, that there were adventurers in the Territories of Mississippi and Orleans who had joined the convention army and who might cause trouble. Claiborne felt it necessary to have a detachment of troops follow him down the river. William King, Governor Claiborne's messenger, was sent to Baton Rouge with a copy of Madison's proclamation and was arrested by the authorities there.[32]

On December 4 Holmes left Washington ahead of Claiborne to go to St. Francisville for conferences with leaders of the Assembly. Arriving on December 6, he learned that resi-

30. *Ibid.*

31. Robert Smith to William C. C. Claiborne, *ibid.*, 396–97.

32. Arthur, *The Story of the West Florida Rebellion*, 133; Claiborne to William King, December 5, 1810, in W. C. C. Claiborne, *Official Letter Books*, V, 79–80.

dents were concerned with "the debt, the land claims and the deserters." Holmes promised immunity for the deserters and pointed out that the United States had always had a liberal land policy with settlers. He said that it was foolish to oppose American authorities and that residents of West Florida need not fear the "fair and friendly negotiation" clause because the United States would never give West Florida back to Spain. He conferred with Governor Skipwith, but was unable to convince him that the United States government was not acting in a high-handed and arbitrary manner. Skipwith left with several members of the Assembly for Baton Rouge where the legislative assembly was to meet the next day.[33]

When Claiborne arrived at Pointe Coupee on December 7, 1810, with two army officers and thirty-three regulars, he was joined by Audley L. Osborn and Governor Holmes. John H. Johnson also crossed the river with a message for Claiborne: "Governor Skipwith had charged me verbally to inform you that he has retired to the fort of Baton Rouge, and rather than surrender the Country unconditionally and without terms, he would, with 20 men only, if a greater force could not be procured surround the Flag Staff and die in defense of the Lone Star Flag!"[34] Claiborne did not reply to this message. Johnson then assured the governor of his own loyalty and said that Claiborne would be welcomed in St. Francisville if he would cross the river. Osborne was sent to ascertain the accuracy of Johnson's statement, and he returned to say that the people would be happy to have Claiborne cross the river. The convention army that had been

33. Cox, *The West Florida Controversy*, 494–500; William C. C. Claiborne to Robert Smith, December 7, 1810, in W. C. C. Claiborne, *Official Letter Books*, V, 47.
34. Arthur, *The Story of the West Florida Rebellion*, 136–37.

dispatched to Mobile had been recalled and had arrived in St. Francisville.[35]

Holmes and Claiborne crossed the river and were received with "great respect" by the people of the town. Escorted by soldiers, Claiborne marched to the middle of the town. The militia made a circle around the flagstaff with Claiborne in the middle. The proclamation by President Madison was read, and Claiborne made a brief speech. Then the West Florida flag was lowered and the American flag raised on December 7, 1810.[36]

But the surrender of Baton Rouge promised to be more difficult. Holmes went ahead again to try to conciliate Skipwith, who resented not only the manner in which the occupation was taking place but also the fact that the title to West Florida was still in doubt. He felt that the successful rebellion had given the Republic of West Florida a fair and legitimate title to the territory.[37]

Just before he reached Baton Rouge, Holmes sent messengers to see if he might enter the town. King, Claiborne's first messenger, had been arrested but subsequently released by Skipwith. Holmes was kept waiting a short time and then allowed to proceed to Baton Rouge.[38]

After a conference with Governor Skipwith and Captain Ballinger, it was agreed that there would be no resistance when Governor Claiborne landed. Holmes again gave assurance that deserters would not be punished. When they left the conference, word was brought that five American gun-

35. *Ibid.*, 140; William C. C. Claiborne to Robert Smith, December 7, 1810, in W. C. C. Claiborne, *Official Letter Books*, V, 48; Cox, *The West Florida Controversy*, 500.

36. Arthur, *The Story of the West Florida Rebellion*, 137; Cox, *The West Florida Controversy*, 501–502.

37. Cox, *The West Florida Controversy*, 502–504.

38. *Ibid.*

boats had come down the river; by the time Holmes could get to the landing, Colonel Leonard Covington had landed 245 men. Governor Holmes informed the colonel that he would meet with no resistance and gave a letter to Claiborne from Fulwar Skipwith in which the former governor expressed his gratification at the annexation of West Florida but protested the methods used by Claiborne "as an outrage against the flag and constitution of West Florida." Skipwith also requested amnesty for those who might be deserters and asked that the flag of West Florida be treated with respect. Skipwith would not give the order to lower the flag; neither would he give an order that would lead to the shedding of American blood.

Claiborne requested that the troops evacuate Fort San Carlos at half past two and surrender their arms. Precisely at the designated time, the convention army of four hundred men marched out of the fort and saluted the flag of the Republic of West Florida for the last time. "The whole force of four hundred men . . . with their muskets at shoulder, gathered about the white staff in the center of the parade in the fort. As the Lone Star descended the pole the muskets crashed out a volley. Then, in obedience to low commands the men tramped out of the gates and formed in line in the esplanade, stacked their arms, laid off their accoutrements, and were marched by the officers into the village and dismissed."[39]

At three o'clock, United States troops under the command of Colonel Leonard Covington marched into the fort, formed a square around the flagstaff, and when Claiborne gave the command, a color sergeant raised the Stars and Stripes over

39. Arthur, *The Story of the West Florida Rebellion*, 139, 140; Cox, *The West Florida Controversy*, 504–505.

West Florida. It was saluted by a "volley from the muskets and twenty-one measured blasts from a field piece." Claiborne wrote later that "peaceable possession was taken on the 10th of the Town, Fort and District of Baton Rouge in the name and behalf of the United States."[40]

Former governor Fulwar Skipwith assured the new governor that he could rely on the American and French population. He also recommended the convention troops if Claiborne should need their assistance. Claiborne wrote to the secretary of state that "a more heterogeneous mass of good and evil was never before met in the same extent of territory." He added that the most influential members of the convention were friends of the United States, but there were others who "are hand and heart devoted to the British interests and whenever occasion favors it, by their acts [they] evince their dislike of American institutions."[41]

The new governor of West Florida, now a part of the Territory of Orleans, knew that in Baton Rouge he was faced with an almost unique situation. Not counting the Americans, the population was a mixture of French, English, and Spanish. These Europeans exhibited all the antipathies and factional loyalties of their counterparts on the Continent. Baton Rouge was a microcosm of the larger situation in Europe. In less than half a century it had changed hands five times, and except for seventy-four short days when it was a republic, the territory had been a pawn in the game played by England, France and Spain. The people were expected to switch their loyalties from one monarch to another with each move. Baton Rouge at this time was a frontier village, and

40. Arthur, *The Story of the West Florida Rebellion*, 140–41; William C. C. Claiborne to Robert Smith, December 12, 1810, in W. C. C. Claiborne, *Official Letter Books*, V, 53.

41. Cox, *The West Florida Controversy*, 507; Arthur, *The Story of the West Florida Rebellion*, 140.

in due time the frontier would affect the national character of the population. In the meantime, Claiborne had to deal with a people who had been affected by European court intrigues. Settlers had come to this area for many reasons—not all of them admirable. Independent and belligerent, they would be quick to claim their "rights" as American citizens, and they would be difficult to govern. Claiborne would find that when West Floridians used the phrase "free and independent" it was more descriptive of the character of the people than of the state of the republic. Because of recent history, they were also more sophisticated than the usual citizens of a frontier territory.

The plantation system, on which the economy of the District of Baton Rouge was based, provided more leisure time in which leaders could discuss the various national and international problems that arose. Politics was discussed in plantation homes after dinner, and one can imagine that Skipwith, with his many years of service as consul behind him, could talk with authority of the political strengths and weaknesses of France. Others, with equal authority, could discuss the Spanish, English, and American systems.

Now that West Florida was a part of the Louisiana purchase and had been occupied as such, it would seem simple enough to incorporate it as a separate territory or as part of the Mississippi or Louisiana territories. But disposition of West Florida was not so simple. The loyalties of the people were divided between Spain, England, France, the United States, the Republic of West Florida, Mississippi Territory, and the Territory of Orleans.

West Floridians could see through the diplomatic maneuvers of American statesmen who wished to acquire their territory. They, particularly the American element, pragmatically accepted and understood Jefferson's "gospel of Pan-Americanism" and his willingness to go along with Livingston's argument that West Florida was a part of the Louisiana Purchase. One historian contends that the real credit for acquisition of the area should go to the American pioneers who had settled and developed the land in spite of the Spanish and their intrigues with the Indians. They occupied the territory by peaceful means and caused an "area that physiographically belonged to the United States" to become a part of it politically. And of "commanding influence" were those people who lived in Baton Rouge.[42]

One such commanding figure was Fulwar Skipwith, governor of the Republic of West Florida. A Virginian by birth, he received his first appointment as consul to the West Indian Islands from President George Washington. Later he became consul general to France. Distinguished looking, intelligent, and cosmopolitan, he was well equipped to lead the Republic. His home was Montsanto plantation above Baton Rouge, where he lived until his death in 1839.[43]

General Philemon Thomas, commandant of the convention army, was also a Virginian who ran away from home at seventeen to serve in the Revolutionary War and distinguished himself in the battles of King's Mountain, Eutaw Springs and Guilford Courthouse. He moved to Kentucky and was a delegate to the convention which framed the constitution of the state of Kentucky. Later he served in the Kentucky House of Representatives and in the state Senate. It is interesting to note that he married the daughter of one

42. Cox, *The West Florida Controversy*, 661, 665–68.

43. Arthur, *The Story of the West Florida Rebellion*, 90–91; Henry Bartholomew Cox, *The Parisian American: Fulwar Skipwith of Virginia* (Washington, D.C.: Mount Vernon Publishing Company, 1964), 155–56.

of the dissenting ministers whom Patrick Henry had defended.[44]

Larry Moore, also from Kentucky, was cunning enough to sneak his men into Fort San Carlos and take it with comparative ease. Peter Kemper, a Baptist minister, moved from Virginia in 1800 and settled in Ohio. Three of his seven sons, Nathan, Reuben, and Sam had tried to free West Florida from Spain in the ill-fated Kemper Rebellion of 1804. They were still active after Claiborne took over. These men were among the many prominent Americans in West Florida who were determined to incorporate the territory within the United States.[45]

Following its occupation by the United States several plans were submitted for the disposition of West Florida. "With the seizure justified by vote of Congress, measures for the disposition of the seized territory were in order," wrote Henry Chambers. Senator William B. Giles of Virginia introduced a bill to admit Louisiana as a state and include the region to the Perdido. George M. Troup of Georgia felt that West Florida could not be annexed to the Territory of Orleans because the "area was yet in dispute and subject to negotiation." Another Georgia congressman, William W. Bibb, moved that the disputed area be annexed to the Mississippi Territory or be made a separate government. But Congressman John Rhea of Tennessee argued that West Florida was a part of Louisiana and could not become a part of Mississippi. If it was not a part of Louisiana, then Madison had committed an act of war against Spain. (A representative of Great Britain had written to the American secretary of state

44. *Ibid.*; U.S. Congress, *Biographical Directory of the American Congress, 1774–1971* (Washington, D.C.: Government Printing Office, 1971), 1807.
45. Arthur, *The Story of the Kemper Brothers*, 4.

that "the Act . . . of sending a force to West Florida to secure by arms what was before a subject of friendly negotiation, cannot, I much fear, under any palliation, be considered other than as an act of open hostility against Spain.")[46]

While all this was going on in Washington, the people of West Florida and Mississippi Territory were beginning to make themselves heard on the subject of annexation. In 1811 inhabitants of Mississippi sent a petition to Congress in which they cited the "inconveniences and even oppressions" of a territorial government and asked that Mississippi be admitted as a "free, sovereign and independent state." Since Mississippi did not have the necessary population for state-hood, the petitioners asked that West Florida be joined to their territory. They also stated that this was in accordance with the wishes of the people of West Florida. Then they gave reasons why annexation to Mississippi would be prefer-able. First, many residents of West Florida were Americans by birth and principle, "their political sentiments . . . re-publican, and their political creed—the Federal constitu-tion." The petitioners added that their local interests were the same—as were their agricultural and other pursuits. Finally, it was maintained "that where Nature fixes the boundaries of a state, there ought to be its limits when they do not conflict with its real and substantial interests." They pointed out that nature had prescribed such boundaries— "the Mississippi on the West and the lake Ponchartrain [*sic*] and the shores of the Atlantic on the South and South East." They pleaded to be "politically united to people to whom we are already united by nature."[47]

46. Adams, *History of the United States*, V, 319–25; J. P. Morier to Robert Smith, December 15, 1810, in *American State Papers, Foreign Relations*, III, 399.
47. Petition by the people of the Mississippi territory to the Senate and House, December 27, 1811, in Carter, *Territory of Mississippi*, 1809–1817, VI, 253–54.

These petitioners were, for the most part, Anglo-Saxons
who had originally come from the British Isles, or whose
parents or grandparents had come from there. The names at
the bottom of the petition are familiar to the twentieth-cen-
tury Baton Rougean who reads his daily paper. Culturally
the people of Baton Rouge had much in common with their
Mississippi neighbors. According to Isaac Cox, "The American claim included that portion of the Mississippi delta and
its back country of which Baton Rouge is the natural center.
. . . The Western portion resembled the Natchez district,
with which it made a common physiographic unit. Here
was found the larger part of West Florida's scattered population gathered into considerable communities along the lakes
and as far eastward as the Pearl."[48]

Colonel John Ballinger, with a letter of introduction from
Governor Holmes, went to Washington in 1811 as an official
agent of West Florida so that he might "have an opportunity
of giving correct and useful information in case the affairs of
that part of the country should become a subject of delibera-
tion." He could very well be called the first lobbyist from
Baton Rouge. Holmes wrote that Ballinger possessed an
accurate knowledge of the geography of the area and that he
had "a knowledge of the character and disposition of its inhabitants." Ballinger himself had written earlier, "Some may
propose one thing or another but the Great Mass of the people
Wants [*sic*] nothing more than to become American citizens."[49]

Although there was a move to join West Florida to Mississippi, sentiment in Baton Rouge seemed overwhelmingly in

48. Cox, *The West Florida Controversy*, 4.
49. *Ibid.*, 418–19, 597–99; David Holmes to James Monroe, September 20, 1811, in
Carter (ed.), *The Territory of Mississippi, 1809–1817*, VI of *The Territorial Papers of the
United States* (Washington, D.C.: Government Printing Office, 1938), 224–25.

favor of annexation to the Territory of Orleans even before the West Florida rebellion.[50] If the United States persisted in saying that it was a part of the Louisiana Purchase, then it was already a part of that territory. But, of course, Congress would make the final decision as to which state it would be a part of—Mississippi or Louisiana.

Governor Claiborne, in the meantime, needed to organize a local interim government for West Florida. The president's proclamation was, in essence, government by executive decree in that it provided for a governor, laws, funds, and so forth. But even with all this authority it was necessary to divide West Florida into smaller units for the purpose of administration. The region, which was bounded by the Territory of Mississippi on the north, by what had been the Territory of Orleans on the south, the Mississippi River on the west, and the Perdido River on the east, was divided into four parishes—Feliciana, East Baton Rouge, St. Helena and St. Tammany. The proclamation naming and delimiting these parishes was signed on December 22, 1810.[51]

With administrative units formed for what was now called the county of Feliciana, the governor proceeded to appoint certain local officials. The important and influential political figure, Fulwar Skipwith, refused to serve in any official capacity and retired to Montesano to manage his plantation. But Claiborne was able to appoint two men who would be friendly to the United States and who were, in his words, "capable honest men" who had "acquired the confidence" of the people. George Mather, English by birth but for thirty-five years a resident of the District of Baton Rouge, was appointed judge for the District of Baton Rouge. Dr. Andrew Steele of

50. Cox, *The West Florida Controversy*, 416.
51. Gayarré, *History of Louisiana*, IV, 244; Davis, *Louisiana: A Narrative History*, 173.

Baton Rouge was appointed to the judgeship of Feliciana. Claiborne did not select judges for St. Helena and St. Tammany because, as he said, "there is in that quarter a great scarcity of talent, and the number of virtuous men, I fear, is not as great as I could wish."[52]

There was an immediate outcry against Claiborne's arbitrary assignment of parish boundaries. In the process of dividing the region, he had enlarged Baton Rouge and decreased Feliciana. John H. Johnson and John Rhea wrote Claiborne complaining about the division. The governor, who always tried to conciliate, said, "I have heard with sincere regret that in laying out the parish of Feliciana, I have greatly curtailed its ancient limits and subjected many Citizens to inconvenience by placing them in the bounds of East Baton Rouge." He asked the residents to "furnish him with [their] sentiments on this subject" and added that since he had apparently inconvenienced the residents he would "endeavor to correct the wrong as soon as may be practicable." Later, Claiborne changed the boundary of Feliciana, extending it to the Amite and including what is now West Feliciana. He also added two more parishes—Biloxi and Pascagoula. With the addition of Pascagoula, which extended to the Perdido River, all of West Florida had now been divided into administrative units.[53]

By staying in the county of Feliciana until after Christmas and trying to make the residents understand his position, Governor Claiborne had "won many friends and admirers by his exercise of sound judgment after taking possession of the

52. Arthur, *The Story of the West Florida Rebellion*, 147; William C. C. Claiborne to Robert Smith, December 24, 1810, in W. C. C. Claiborne, *Official Letter Books*, V, 62.

53. William C. C. Claiborne to John Rhea and John H. Johnson, January 31, 1811, in W. C. C. Claiborne, *Official Letter Books*, V, 139–40; Arthur, *The Story of the West Florida Rebellion*, 147; Davis, *Louisiana: A Narrative History*, 173.

late Republic of West Florida, and his course of conciliation did much to heal wounded feelings." He may have been reluctant to leave Baton Rouge because, as he wrote to President Madison, "I set out for New Orleans to encounter . . . all the intrigues . . . and the disappointed Office Hunters, and every Burrite in the Territory." He added that he hoped he would be able to maintain his ground in the face of all his "enemies."[54]

On April 10, 1811, Claiborne established the Seventh Superior Court for the county of Feliciana. Court would be held "in and for the Seventh District, on the First Mondays of March and August, at the town of St. Francisville." Appointed officials for the area were: John H. Johnson, high sheriff of the county of Feliciana; John Rhea, judge of the county of Feliciana; and Dr. Andrew Steele, who was appointed to the judgeship of East Baton Rouge after the resignation of George Mather.[55] Claiborne also appointed officials for the other parishes. Apparently by then he had been able to discover more talent.

Representation in the territorial government at New Orleans was extremely important to residents of West Florida; and, on February 1, 1811, Governor Claiborne issued a writ of election for three representatives from the County of Feliciana to the territorial legislature. Then on February 5, 1811, an act, passed by the territorial legislature and approved by the governor, changed the number of representatives to five—three from Feliciana and East Baton Rouge, one from St. Helena and St. Tammany, and one from Biloxi and Pascagoula. On February 7, 1811, Claiborne issued writs of elec-

54. Arthur, *The Story of the West Florida Rebellion*, 148–49. Arthur's statement that Claiborne left Baton Rouge before Christmas is probably based on a letter dated December 24; but Claiborne wrote other letters from Baton Rouge dated December 27 and 28.
55. *Ibid.*

tion so that elections of these representatives could be held on February 21, 22, and 23.[56]

These parishes, however, were not represented in the territorial assembly even though a legislative act provided for such representation. Stanley C. Arthur states that he was never able to find a "record of such elections being held nor any names of those who might have been chosen to represent the new country." According to Isaac Cox, five members were sent to the Orleans legislature to represent West Florida, but the legislature refused to seat them.[57] One also finds that Colonel John Ballinger wrote on December 26, 1811, to Secretary of State James Monroe that: "the refusal of the Legislature of the Territory of Orleans, at their late session to elect a Representative to Congress, has deprived the people of Feliciana of any legitimate organ of public will on that floor, and feeling as they do both their honor and interest involved in the Radical and Successive political changes which have recently taken place in that Country, they have appointed the undersigned their Special agent to lay before this government their wishes and wants."[58]

Ballinger presented their grievances and requested that a temporary government be set up until "consent can be obtained in a Constitutional way." He said that the people wished to be attached to the new state of Louisiana and protested the idea of becoming attached to the Territory of

56. Claiborne issued a Writ of Election, February 1, 1811, in Carter, *Territory of Orleans, 1803–1812*, IX, 982; Arthur, *The Story of the West Florida Rebellion*, 149–50; William C. C. Claiborne to Robert Smith, February 7, 1811, in W. C. C. Claiborne, *Official Letter Books*, V, 146.

57. Arthur, *The Story of the West Florida Rebellion*, 150; Cox, *The West Florida Controversy*, 576; Claiborne to Smith, February 7, 1811, in W. C. C. Claiborne, *Official Letter Books*, V, 146.

58. John Ballinger to James Monroe, December 26, 1811, in Carter (ed.), *Territory of Orleans*, IX, 964.

Mississippi or the state of Mississippi "should it become one."[59]

Ballinger also complained that the United States military commandant, General Wade Hampton, had misused his authority since being stationed at Baton Rouge. Ballinger said, "He [Hampton] has turned about one-third of the inhabitants of Baton Rouge out of their Houses, on a pretext of its being public land attached to the fort—some of the people were living there previous to the year 1800 and nearly all previous to 1803, the houses were built by the owners not by the public." General Hampton had also been using the Catholic burying ground for the purpose of "burying his dead . . . altho it has been consecrated and used by the Church upwards of Twenty years."[60]

The inhabitants of the county of Feliciana felt that the United States government was not treating fairly "many of our Citizens who made large advances of money, property, and personal service to effect our emancipation from foreign oppression, without any hope of remuneration." One can see by the statements above that the people were becoming restless and very disillusioned with the territorial government. Some felt that they had even less freedom than they had enjoyed when they were Spanish subjects—no representation still, but now they paid taxes. The county of Feliciana was paying for the privilege of being a part of the Territory of Orleans, but it was receiving little in return.[61]

When the enabling act, which would authorize a state constitutional convention for the Territory of Orleans, was

59. *Ibid.*, 966–67.
60. *Ibid.*, 966–70.
61. *Ibid.*, 981; Arthur, *The Story of the West Florida Rebellion*, 150. Arthur states that they were to pay a territorial tax of six thousand dollars plus seventy-five cents a head for each slave.

passed by Congress and signed by the president on February 20, 1811, no provision was made to include West Florida in the new state of Louisiana. Even though West Florida had been annexed to the Territory of Orleans by proclamation and was being governed as a part of the territory, its citizens were not authorized to elect delegates to the constitutional convention.[62]

The people of Baton Rouge and the surrounding parishes were angered, and with just cause. They paid taxes and were obliged to obey the laws as a part of the territory, but were represented neither in the territorial legislature nor in Congress, and now it appeared they would have no part in the writing of the state constitution and the admission of Louisiana to the Union. Once more residents were on the verge of insurrection, and when the people of Feliciana rose on the morning of March 17, they found the Lone Star flag of the Republic of West Florida waving once more over the town of St. Francisville. General Hampton came from Baton Rouge and "immediately called on the civil officer and stated that he considered the flag flying an insult to his government." He stated that if the flag were not taken down that day he would order a detachment of troops to lower it on the following day. The civil officer, realizing the seriousness of the flag-raising incident, ordered the flag down, and this order was carried out immediately.[63]

Writing of the flag-raising incident to Secretary of State Robert Smith, Governor Claiborne said:

I learn that some of the Inhabitants of St. Francisville in Feliciana have lately conducted themselves, very improperly and that

62. Gayarré, *History of Louisiana*, IV, 268.
63. Arthur, *The Story of the West Florida Rebellion*, 151; William C. C. Claiborne to Robert Smith, March 22, in W. C. C. Claiborne, *Official Letter Books*, V, 187–88.

among other acts of great indiscretion, they have reared [*sic*] the Florida flag. It however was soon taken down (without producing any serious commotion) by the orders of Genl. Hampton; and the Pavilion of the U. States again displayed. The people of Feliciana are greatly dissatisfied at the proposition made in Congress to seperate [*sic*] them from the Territory of Orleans. It occasions many good Citizens to believe that their political destiny is yet uncertain; and the base and designing are incessant in their efforts to promote discontent.[64]

On the day following the flag incident, some of the same revolutionaries who had stormed Baton Rouge when it was taken from the Spanish were supposed to have buried the flag of West Florida in a "private lot with great ceremony."[65]

As the summer of 1811 wore on, people were becoming more impatient. Judge William D. Nicholson of East Baton Rouge Parish resigned his position in August after serving less than a year. Newspapers kept the problem of Congress and their conduct toward West Florida ever before the public. Governor Claiborne said of one such publication: "A News-paper here, called "The Time Piece," had assumed a shape by no means calculated to conciliate the affections of the people toward the government. The Editor possesses Genius, But neither Judgment or discretion. This paper teems with abuse of Congress & their conduct toward [Louisiana?] is represented as wrongful and oppressive. That these publications have made injurious impressions is certain."[66]

Perhaps the editor of this St. Francisville paper had done

64. William C. C. Claiborne to Robert Smith, March 22, 1811, in W. C. C. Claiborne, *Official Letter Books*, V, 187–88.

65. Arthur, *The Story of the West Florida Rebellion*, 151.

66. Civil Appointments made in the Territory of Orleans, 1811, in Carter (ed.), *Territory of Orleans*, IX, 984; Arthur, *The Story of the West Florida Rebellion*, 152; William C. C. Claiborne to James Monroe, September 2, 1811, in W. C. C. Claiborne, *Official Letter Books*, V, 352–53.

no more than express publicly what people were saying privately.

Claiborne, like his predecessor de Lassus, had reason to fear any "meetings" of residents of East Baton Rouge and Feliciana parishes. One such meeting was to take place on September 26, 1811, to celebrate the capture of the fort at Baton Rouge. Claiborne was hopeful that Judge John Rhea of Feliciana would have a quieting effect on the hotheads. The governor wrote to James Monroe that Rhea was a "prudent, judicious, well-disposed man, and seems to be much attached to the government of the United States."[67]

Claiborne visited the people of Feliciana in September and "persuaded the citizens to remain calm and compel the impatient to follow suit." At that time it was simply a matter of trying to keep things quiet until the constitutional convention could meet and subsequent action in Washington by the Congress could be accomplished. General Hampton, with headquarters at Baton Rouge, could suppress any threatening activity that might take place in the surrounding territory, which, once more, was becoming a "storm center" for rebellion. There would be another meeting at St. John's Plains in Feliciana in December. In the meantime, Claiborne continued his policy of reassuring the people of West Florida that the "President had nothing more at heart, than the happiness of the people of West Florida and their permanent connection with the American family."[68] Claiborne's actions were characterized by patience and sincere friendship for the West Floridians. From his letters, one gets the feeling that he was more in sympathy with the Anglo-Saxon element in

67. Arthur, *The Story of the West Florida Rebellion*, 152–53.
68. *Ibid*.

West Florida than with the Creole element in New Orleans.

Of the many letters, petitions, and memorials sent to Washington by various officials and private citizens, one memorial deserves special attention. It was presented to the House of Representatives on March 17, 1812, by the residents of the County of Feliciana. It read:

> that your memorialists having been lately incorporated into the American Union, as is well known to your honorable body, and at the same time attached to the said territory as a part of Louisiana, have viewed with much regret the provisions of a late act of Congress authorizing a state government within the said territory of Orleans, with such limits and boundaries as will exclude your memorialists, and separate them entirely from the state so about to be formed. While we declare our entire confidence in the upright intentions of your honorable body, we beg leave to remonstrate in the strongest terms, against a measure which we humbly conceive to be not only an infringement of our rights, but injurious to our fellow citizens of the said territory of Orleans, and to the interests of the United States. . . . Your memorialists pray . . . that the act . . . may be so amended that the said county of Feliciana may be included within the state so to be formed and admitted to the union.[69]

Although the enabling act had been passed in February, 1811, it was near the end of the year before the constitutional convention convened on the first Monday of November in New Orleans. With Julian Poydras as permanent chairman, the forty-three delegates started writing a state constitution that would be acceptable to Congress. It was completed and adopted on January 22, 1812.[70]

The next day, January 23, 1812, Alexander Porter re-

69. Memorial to Congress from the inhabitants of Feliciana, March 17, 1812, in Carter (ed.), *Territory of Orleans*, IX, 1007–1008.
70. Chambers, *A History of Louisiana*, I, 507.

ported a memorial which had been prepared requesting the annexation of West Florida to the state of Louisiana.[71] The memorial by the "Representatives of the People of the Territory of Orleans in Convention assembled" stated, very respectfully, that the representatives had "turned their eyes toward that portion" of the country from the Mississippi to the Perdido. They felt that it was in the real interest of everyone concerned that this region be attached to the new state of Louisiana "as soon as the Arrangements of the Government in relation to it will permit." After enumerating the reasons West Florida should be a part of Louisiana, the memorialists added that, though they considered "the Annexation of Florida to this Territory, as a subject of First Importance to its future Security and Prosperity," that this was not to be interpreted as a condition for accepting statehood. They were prepared to accept "that rank without such annexation as Speedily as possible." It was signed by Poydras as president of the convention. This memorial was referred to the Committee of the Whole House on the Bill for Admission of Louisiana on March 19, 1812. Having adopted this memorial, the constitutional convention adjourned January 28, 1812, to await the verdict of the Congress of the United States.[72]

The bill to make Louisiana a state passed both houses of Congress without the clause annexing West Florida, and it was approved by President Madison on April 8, 1812, with the proviso that Louisiana would become a state on April 30.[73] Immediately another bill was passed to enlarge the

71. Gayarré, *History of Louisiana*, IV, 273.

72. Petition to Congress by the Territorial Convention, January 23, 1812, in Carter (ed.), *Territory of Orleans*, IX, 990–92; Gayarré, *History of Louisiana*, IV, 273.

73. Chambers, *A History of Louisiana*, I, 507.

state of Louisiana to include part of West Florida. This bill was approved April 14, 1812. It provided that:

> All the tract of the country comprehended within the following bounds, to wit: Beginning at the junction of the Iberville River, or Bayou Manchac, with the Mississippi, then along the middle of Iberville, the river Amite, and of the Lakes Maurepas and Ponchartrain [*sic*] to the eastern mouth of the Pearl River; to the thirty-first degree of North Latitude; then along the said degree of latitude; thence down the said river shall become and form a part of the State of Louisiana.

This enlargement was approved by the state legislature on August 4, 1812, and on the following day the legislature granted three senators and six representatives to the area that had been incorporated into the new state of Louisiana.[74]

Governor Claiborne, now an elected official, gave his inaugural address on July 31, 1812, but East Baton Rouge, Feliciana, St. Helena, and St. Tammany parishes had taken no part in the election of the first governor.[75]

For nine years the people of West Florida had been in an untenable political situation. Badly governed by Spain and claimed at the same time by the United States, the citizens, thoroughly frustrated, had rebelled and set up their own republic. They had scarcely begun to have a semblance of a government when the republic was occupied by the United States army. West Florida was then considered a part of the Territory of Orleans, yet its inhabitants had none of the rights and privileges enjoyed by other inhabitants of the territory. Respect for civil authority had decreased, due in part to the feeling that West Floridians had been treated unfairly by the reigning power, Spain, until 1810 and after

---

74. Gayarré, *History of Louisiana*, IV, 280–81; Chambers, *A History of Louisiana*, I, 507; Martin, *History of Louisiana*, 354–55.

75. Gayarré, *History of Louisiana*, IV, 283.

by the United States. Governor Claiborne recognized this problem and, in a message on August 14, 1812, to the state legislature, said: "On turning my attention to the interior situation of the State, I perceive with regret, that within the parishes of Feliciana, Baton Rouge, St. Helena & St. Tammany (which have recently been annexed to Louisiana) the Civil Authority has become so weakened & relaxed, that the laws have lost much of their influence, & in the parish of St. Tammany particularly are scarcely felt.—I advise therefore Gentlemen, that such provisions as you shall think proper to prescribe for these parishes, may be passed with all convenient dispatch."[76]

One of the provisions that the legislature thought fit to prescribe was to give the parishes representation in the assembly. Since 1810 West Floridians had not been permitted to have a voice in the government. All acts passed with reference to that area had been legislated without either the consent or dissent in a legislative body of the people involved.

In November, Claiborne called the legislature into extraordinary session for the purpose of choosing electors to vote for the president and vice-president of the United States, and in a joint meeting the Senate and House chose Julian Poydras, Philemon Thomas, and Stephen A. Hopkins.[77]

Philemon Thomas, the first official representative from West Florida to the nation's capital, was a resident of Baton Rouge. This elector was not Spanish, French, or English, but an American, born in Virginia, who had fought in two successful revolutions, first in the American Revolution and then in the West Florida Rebellion. Claiborne called him the

76. Speech by Claiborne to the legislature at New Orleans, August 14, 1812, in W. C. C. Claiborne, *Official Letter Books*, VI, 161–62.
77. Gayarré, *History of Louisiana*, IV, 286.

"Ajax of the Revolution" (West Florida), and Stanley C. Arthur described him as "Baptist, tall with a powerful frame, with red hair and clear blue eyes, and known to be the possessor of unquestioned courage."[78] Another writer said:

> Thomas was most conspicuous and most remarkable. He was almost entirely without education but was gifted with great good sense, a bold and honest soul, and a remarkable natural eloquence. His manner was always natural and genial. . . . The character in his face, the flash of his eye, the remarkable self-possession, the natural dignity of deportment, and his great good sense, attracted and won everyone. In all his transactions, he was the same plain honest man . . . rigidly stern in his morals, but eminently charitable to the shortcomings of others.[79]

Perhaps it was a good omen for Baton Rouge and for West Florida that a native American was chosen the first official representative. Philemon Thomas, a product of the American frontier, could hold his own among other Americans. He, along with other Baton Rougeans, had been denied the rights and privileges of other citizens of the Territory of Louisiana. And, as a Virginia-born American, he felt this keenly. He spoke up for his constituents in the Louisiana legislature where, at least on one occasion, he blocked the election of a United States senator because he felt that General Thomas Posey, the candidate, did not meet the residence requirements. According to Governor Claiborne, Thomas blocked Posey's election without vilifying him.[80]

The progression of the Republic of West Florida to a part

78. Arthur, *The Story of the West Florida Rebellion*, 92; William C. C. Claiborne to Robert Smith, December 17, 1810, in W. C. C. Claiborne, *Official Letter Books*, V, 56.

79. W. H. Sparks, *The Memories of Fifty Years* (Macon, Ga.: J. W. Burke & Co., 1872), 393–94.

80. William C. C. Claiborne to Thomas Posey, January 25, 1812, in W. C. C. Claiborne, *Official Letter Books*, VI, 210.

of the state of Louisiana had been accomplished, but for those who had wished so fervently to become a part of the United States the triumph was tinged with bitterness and distrust. Fulwar Skipwith, governor of the Republic of West Florida, had been angered because of the method used to achieve this end. Yet, the president of the United States could hardly do otherwise, if, as it was claimed, West Florida was a part of the Louisiana Purchase. More seeds of dissension had been sown in a fertile soil of disunity. Easily angered and often belligerent, the various factions, British, Spanish, French, and American, would no doubt continue to be politically active. Distrust of a government born in 1810, when Baton Rouge was subjected to military occupation, would continue. To many idealistic people of Baton Rouge, a beautiful dream had somehow become tarnished by political reality.

Baton Rouge and West Florida comprised perhaps the first example in American history of overt territorial aggrandizement, accompanied by a sense of moral self-righteousness. West Florida had been important to Spain, England and France for various reasons, but after the United States began to have growing pains, its need for territory became intense. Soon the government of the United States was expressing the wishes of its people when it started maneuvering to obtain both East and West Florida. As it happened, the United States obtained West Florida first.

One must not underestimate the power of the American frontiersmen who were gradually moving into the disputed area. In West Florida, American settlers began to feel that Spain had no right to try to rule Americans on this continent. The Americans were there; they built homes and developed the land, and, therefore, it was "right" that West Florida should be a part of the United States. Against this rationalization, aggressiveness, and self-righteousness, a foreign nation far removed from the scene had little defense. According to Thomas Andrew Bailey, West Florida had "become ripe for the plucking."[81] And the American government did just that.

Thus did Baton Rouge begin its national history as a part of the United States. The thriving little town of 1812 was a far cry from the cluster of Indian huts found by Iberville. The years from 1699 to 1812 left their mark on the city. Influenced by its various colonial overlords, French, English, and Spanish, Baton Rouge has a unique personality. One finds a certain Anglo-Saxon energy and abruptness tempered by a trace of Gallic charm and a Spanish love of organization. An apparently leisurely pace, a remnant of its plantation economy, is deceiving, because Baton Rougeans march eagerly to the double time of modern commerce and industry. The energy needed for this quickened pace may well have its source in the broad mixture of nationalities and races which resulted in a kind of hybrid strength. Indeed, Baton Rouge is all the more fascinating because of its varied background and unique colonial history.

81. Bailey, *A Diplomatic History of the American People*, 165.

Bibliography

PRIMARY SOURCES

Manuscripts

"Archives of the Spanish Government of West Florida." 18 vols. Office of Clerk of Court, Baton Rouge. Translation and transcription by Works Progress Administration, 1937–38.

D'Artaguette, Diron. "Journal of Diron d'Artaguette." Original in Archives des Colonies, Paris, France. Film 89 in Tulane University Library, New Orleans.

"Baton Rouge." Old File, National Archives. Copy in State Land Office, Baton Rouge.

Maps

D'Anville, S. "Carte de la Louisianne par le S. d'Anville, 1732." Louisiana State University Library, Baton Rouge.

"Course of the River Mississippi from the Balise to Fort Chartres." Taken on an expedition to the Illinois in the latter part of the Year 1765 by Lieut. Ross of the 34th Regiment. Copy in the map case of East Baton Parish Library, Baton Rouge.

"Plan of the proposed New Town also the proposed Cut from the Mississippi to the Iberville." Also an untitled map on this film showing the width and depth of the Iberville River in 1767. Original in the British Museum, London. Copy in Louisiana State Archives and Records Commission, Baton Rouge.

"Province de Louisianne, 1743." Louisiana Room, Louisiana State University Library, Baton Rouge.

Published Material

American State Papers. Foreign Relations. III. Washington, D.C.: Gales and Seaton, 1832.

———. *Public Lands.* II. Washington, D.C.: Gales and Seaton, 1834.

Annals of the Congress of the United States, 1st Congress to the End of 1st Session of the

18th Congress, 1789–1824. 42 vols. Washington, D.C.: Gales and Seaton, 1834–56.

Bartram, William. *Travels Through North & South Carolina, Georgia, East & West Florida*. Philadelphia: James & Johnson, 1791.

Beer, William. "Early Census Tables of Louisiana." *Louisiana Historical Quarterly*, XIII (April, 1930), 205–29.

"British Proclamation of October 7, 1763." *Louisiana Historical Quarterly*, XIII (October, 1930), 610–16.

Carter, Clarence Edwin, ed. *The Territory of Orleans, 1803–1812*. Vol. IX of *The Territorial Papers of the United States*. Washington, D.C.: Government Printing Office, 1940.

————. *The Territory of Mississippi, 1809–1817*, Vol. VI of *The Territorial Papers of the United States*. Washington, D.C.: Government Printing Office, 1938.

Charlevoix, Pierre F.-X. de. *History and General Description of New France*. 6 vols. Chicago: Loyola University Press, 1962. French edition published in Paris, 1744.

Claiborne, William Charles Cole. *Official Letter Books of W. C. C. Claiborne, 1801–1816*. 6 vols. Jackson: Mississippi State Department of Archives and History, 1917.

Du Ru, Paul. *Journal of Paul du Ru*. Chicago: Caxton Club, 1934.

French, Benjamin F., ed. *Historical Collections of Louisiana and Florida*. Second Series. New York: Albert Mason, 1875.

La Harpe, Jean-Baptiste Benard de. *Historical Journal of the Settlement of the French in Louisiana*. Lafayette: University of Southwestern Louisiana, 1971.

Livingston, Robert. *The Original Letters of Robert R. Livingston, 1801–1803*. New Orleans: Louisiana Historical Society, 1953.

Maduell, Charles R. Jr. (comp. and trans.). *The Census Tables for the French Colony of Louisiana from 1699 through 1732*. Baltimore: Genealogical Publishing Company, Inc., 1972.

McWilliams, Richebourg Gaillard, ed. *Fleur de Lys and Calumet: Being the Pénicaut Narrative of French Adventure in Louisiana*. Baton Rouge: Louisiana State University Press, 1953.

"Minutes of the First Session of the Assembly of West Florida." *Louisiana Historical Quarterly*, XXII (April, 1939), 311–84.

Nasatir, A. P., ed. "Government Employees and Salaries in Spanish Louisiana." *Louisiana Historical Quarterly*, XXIX (October, 1946), 885–1040.

Padgett, James A., ed. "Commission, Orders and Instructions Issued to George Johnstone, British Governor of West Florida, 1763–1767." *Louisiana Historical Quarterly*, XXI (October, 1938), 1020–68.

————. "Official Records of the West Florida Revolution and the Republic." *Louisiana Historical Quarterly*, XXI (July, 1938), 685–805.

————. "The West Florida Revolution of 1810, as Told in the Letters of John Rhea, Fulwar Skipwith, Reuben Kemper and Others." *Louisiana Historical Quarterly*, XXI (January, 1938), 77–202.

Rowland, Dunbar. *Mississippi Provincial Archives, 1763–1766. English Dominion*. Vol. I. Nashville: Press of the Brandon Printing Company, 1911.

Rowland, Dunbar, and Albert Godfrey Sanders, eds. *Mississippi Provincial Archives, 1704–1743, French Dominion*. 3 vols. Jackson: Press of the Mississippi Department of Archives and History, 1927–1932.

Rowland, Eron. *Life, Letters and Papers of William Dunbar*. Jackson: Press of the Mississippi Historical Society, 1930.

Thwaites, Reuben Gold, ed. *The Jesuit Relations and Allied Documents: Travels and Explorations of the Jesuit Missionaries in New France, 1610–1791*. 73 vols. Cleveland: Burrows Brothers Company, 1896–1901.

"Trial of Mary Glass for Murder, 1780." *Louisiana Historical Quarterly*, VI (October, 1923), 591–654.

"West Florida—Documents Covering a Royal Land Grant and Other Land Transactions on the Mississippi and Amite Rivers During the English Rule." *Louisiana Historical Quarterly*, XII (October, 1929), 630–44.

SECONDARY SOURCES

Manuscripts

Miller, Wilbert James. "The Spanish Commandant of Baton Rouge, 1779–1795." M.A. thesis, Louisiana State University, 1965.

Books

Adams, Henry. *History of the United States*. 10 vols. New York: Charles Scribner and Sons, 1889–91.

Arthur, Stanley C. *The Story of the Kemper Brothers*. St. Francisville, La.: *Democrat*, 1933. Reprinted from the weekly *Democrat*, published on July 8, 15, 22, 29, 1933.

————. *The Story of the West Florida Rebellion*. St. Francisville, La.: *Democrat*, 1935.

Bailey, Thomas Andrew. *A Diplomatic History of the American People*. New York: Appleton-Century-Crofts, 1964.

Baudier, Roger. *The Catholic Church in Louisiana*. New Orleans: A. W. Hyatt, 1939.

Bemis, Samuel Flagg. *A Diplomatic History of the United States*. Rev. ed.; New York: Henry Holt and Company, 1942.

Burson, Caroline Maud. *The Stewardship of Don Esteban Miró, 1782–1792*. New Orleans: American Printing Company, Ltd., 1940.

Caughey, John Walton, *Bernardo de Gálvez in Louisiana, 1776–1783*. Berkeley: University of California Press, 1934.

Chambers, Henry Edward. *A History of Louisiana*. 3 vols. New York: American Historical Society, Inc., 1925.

Claiborne, John F. H. *Mississippi as a Province, Territory, and State*. Baton Rouge: Louisiana State University Press, 1964.

Cox, Henry Bartholomew. *The Parisian American: Fulwar Skipwith of Virginia*. Washington, D.C.: Mount Vernon Publishing Company, 1964.

Cox, Isaac Joslin. *The West Florida Controversy, 1798–1803*. Gloucester, Mass.: Peter Smith, 1967. Reprint of the Albert Shaw Lectures on Diplomatic History, 1912, first published by Johns Hopkins Press, 1918.

Davis, Edwin Adams. *Louisiana: A Narrative History*. Baton Rouge: Claitor's, 1965.

Deiler, J. Hanno. *The Settlement of the German Coast of Louisiana and the Creoles of German Descent*. Philadelphia: Americana Germanica Press, 1909.

Doyle, Elisabeth Joan. *A Guide to Archival Materials Held by the Catholic Diocese of Baton Rouge*. Baton Rouge: Department of History and Archives of the Catholic Diocese, 1964.

Favrot, J. St. Clair. *Tales of Our Town*. Baton Rouge: Louisiana National Bank, 1973.

Gassler, Francis Leon. *History of St. Joseph's Church*. Marrero, La.: Hope Haven Press, 1943.

Gayarré, Charles Étienne Arthur. *History of Louisiana*. 4 vols. Reprint; Gretna, La.: Pelican Publishing Company, 1965.

Giraud, Marcel. *A History of French Louisiana*. Translated by Joseph C. Lambert. Vol. I. Baton Rouge: Louisiana State University Press, 1974.

Holmes, Jack D. L. *Gayoso: The Life of a Spanish Governor in the Mississippi Valley, 1789–1799*. Baton Rouge: Louisiana State University Press, 1965.

————. *The 1779 "Marcha De Galvez": Louisiana's Giant Step Forward in the American Revolution*. Baton Rouge Bicentennial Corporation, 1974.

James, James Alton. *Oliver Pollock: The Life and Times of an Unknown Patriot*. Freeport, N.Y.: Books for Libraries Press, 1970. Reprint of 1937 edition.

Johnson, Cecil. *British West Florida, 1763–1783*. New York: Archon, 1971.

Lauvrière, Emile. *Histoire de la Louisiane Française, 1673–1939*. Baton Rouge: Louisiana State University Press, 1940.

Le Page du Pratz, A. S. *The History of Louisiana*. London: T. Becket, 1774.

Martin, François-Xavier. *The History of Louisiana from the Earliest Period*. Reprint; Gretna, La.: Pelican Publishing Company, 1963.

McGinty, Garnie William. *A History of Louisiana*. New York: Exposition Press, 1951.

Phelps, Albert. *Louisiana: A Record of Expansion*. Boston: Houghton Mifflin Company, 1905.

Robertson, James Alexander. *Louisiana Under the Rule of Spain, France, and the United States 1785–1807*. 2 vols. Cleveland: Arthur H. Clark Company, 1911.

Rowland, Dunbar. *History of Mississippi*. 2 vols. Jackson: S. J. Clarke Publishing Company, 1925.

Sparks, W. H. *The Memories of Fifty Years*. Macon, Ga.: J. W. Burke & Company, 1872, pp. 393–94.

Swanton, John R. *Indians of the Southeastern United States*. Washington, D.C.: Government Printing Office, 1946.

Williamson, Frederick William, and George T. Goodman, eds. *Eastern Louisiana: A History of the Watershed of the Ouachita River and the Florida Parishes*. Shreveport: Louisiana Historical Record Association, 1939.

Articles

Albrecht, Andrew C. "The Origin and Early Settlement of Baton Rouge, Louisiana." *Louisiana Historical Quarterly*, XXVIII (January, 1945), 5–68.

"Baton Rouge" from the *Old File*, National Archives, Washington, D.C. Copy.

Burns, Francis P. "West Florida and the Louisiana Purchase," *Louisiana Historical Quarterly*, XV (July, 1932), 397–99.

Favrot, J. St. Clair. "Baton Rouge, the Historic Capital of Louisiana." *Louisiana Historical Quarterly*, XII (October, 1929), 611–29.

Johnson, Cecil. "The Distribution of Land in British West Florida." *Louisiana Historical Quarterly*, XVI (October, 1933), 539–53.

Liljegren, Ernest R. "Jacobinism in Spanish Louisiana, 1792–1797." *Louisiana Historical Quarterly*, XXII (January, 1939), 47–97.

Parkhurst, Helen. "Don Pedro Favrot, a Creole Pepys." *Louisiana Historical Quarterly*, XXVII (July, 1945), 679–734.

Read, William A. "Istrouma." *Louisiana Historical Quarterly*, XIV (October, 1931), 503–15.

Scroggs, William. "Origin of the Name of Baton Rouge." *Proceedings of the Historical Society of East and West Baton Rouge, 1916–1917*. Louisiana State University, 1917. I, 20–24.

"West Florida—The Capture of Baton Rouge by Gálvez, September 21st, 1779." *Louisiana Historical Quarterly*, XII (April, 1929), 255–65.

Newspapers

Baton Rouge *Morning Advocate*, October 14, 1965.

Index

Acadians, 60

"Accadian Country," 34

Agriculture: Houmas', 2; on concession, 12, 16; livestock, 20, 55; plantation system, 26; products, 31, 55; mentioned, 19, 20, 80

"Ajax of the Revolution," 134. *See also* Thomas, Philemon

Alexander, Harry, 50

Alleghenies, 69

American gunboats, 107, 114–15

Americans: invade West Florida, 33; Dunbar describes, 35–36; with Gálvez, 37; lip-service to Spain, 65; on Mississippi River, 71; fear Napoleon, 73; as pioneers, 69, 116–18, 135

Amite River, 42, 78, 123

Anglo-Saxons: religion, 43, 63; ideas of government, 41, 73; in French Revolution, 60; Americans and, 64; Mississippians and, 121; Claiborne and, 129; influence of, 136

Argote, Antonio, 61

Articles of Capitulation, 39–40

Assembly of West Florida. *See* Government

Avery, Dudley, L., 108

Baker, Joshua G., 86

Ballinger, John: commands Convention troops, 94, 100; guards fort at Baton Rouge, 107; conference on surrender, 114; goes to Washington, 121; writes secretary of state, 125–26

Baptists, 76, 119, 134

Barcelona, Cirillo de, 52

Barrow, William, 84, 85, 86, 90, 107

Baton Rouge: discovery of site, 1, 9; cypress tree vs. red pole theory, 8, 9; abandoned, 16–20; as point of reference, 17; British take possession of, 21, 22; warehouse at, 25; Dunbar at, 29, 31; and American Revolution, 32–39; government under Spain, 48–49; in French Revolution, 60, 61; military importance of, 41, 63, 65; rebellion, 76–96 *passim*; United States Army occupies, 114–16; mentioned, 2, 6, 7

Baton Rouge, District of: Grand Pré commands, 42; combined with post, 49

Baton Rouge Bayou, 7

Baton Rouge Reach, 7

Baton Rouge Redoubt. *See* Fort New Richmond

Battle of Baton Rouge. 36–41 *passim*

Bayagoulas, 2, 4, 6

Bayou Garrison, 7

Bayou Manchac, 7, 22, 23, 25, 80

Bayou Monte Sano, 7, 27

Bayou Sara, 76, 77, 78, 83, 90, 93

Beauregard, Elias, 59

Beauregard Town, 59

Berges, Francisco de, 49

Bibb, William W., 119

Bienville, Jean Baptiste le Moyne, Sieur de, 4, 11, 19, 69, 70

Biloxi, 17, 19, 123, 124

Blacks: on concession, 12, 13; at Pointe Coupee, 17; to West Florida, 25; and Gálvez, 37, 39; defend fort, 38; owned slaves, 58; outnumbered whites, 65

Blanc, Antoine, 53

Blockade by United States, 80

Blomart, John, 44

Blufflands, 1, 5, 6, 8, 60

143